THE PA

PAUL HARRIS

THE PANTOMIME BOOK

THE ONLY KNOWN COLLECTION OF PANTOMIME JOKES AND SKETCHES IN CAPTIVITY

WITH A FOREWORD BY
ROY HUDD

PETER OWEN
LONDON & CHESTER SPRINGS

PETER OWEN PUBLISHERS
73 Kenway Road London SW5 ORE
Peter Owen books are distributed in the USA by
Dufour Editions Inc. Chester Springs PA 19425–0007

First published in Great Britain 1996
© Paul Harris 1996

ISBN 0–7206–1013–3

A catalogue record for this book is available from the British Library

Printed and made in Great Britain by Biddles
of Guildford and King's Lynn

CONTENTS

FOREWORD

It's nineteen sixty. I'm at the first read through of my very first professional panto. Introductions are made. The musical director stops coughing for just long enough to insert another Capstan full strength. The director gazes longingly out of the window in a pubwards direction and the principal artistes get down to the task in hand.

The principal girl is young and pretty, the principal boy, I'm sure, has great legs if she wasn't clad from head to toe in mink and the odds and sods join in with the cheers and boos. I watch the star comics in awe. They all seem to have Crombie overcoats draped over their shoulders and large cigars in their hands. The character man (Evil) and the soubrette (Good) speak their lines boldly and well and then on come the comedians. You would never know these dour, gruff old men were the harbingers of joy. They mumble through the few lines that are written down, make loud unscripted comments about each other's capacity for booze and crumpet while still attempting to 'spot the goer' from the sixteen nubile girl dancers. Then, suddenly, the read through, which has taken all of an hour, is over. The dancers disappear to a nearby gymnasium, the musical director lights another fag and retires to 'do some dots' and the comics pull their chairs into a circle. 'Now,' says the top of the bill, 'I'll be doing the magic hat, the balloon ballet, the haunted house and my spesh in the ballroom, with . . . [the cigar waves in my direction] . . . him!' The number two comic chips in, 'You could do the pheasant gag with me as well' – me again! 'We'll need a third for the Little Bit of Heaven gag,' from the double act, 'he could handle that.' Me. I'm now in about seven different scenes none of which are in the script! There are only blank pages with the mysterious words GAG HERE typed in the centre.

I start to panic. These people are speaking a foreign language – front cloths, two handers, ghost gags and joey-joeys. The panto was, for me, a real baptism of fire. I tried so hard to make them all think I was an old panto hand but eventually had to own up I didn't know any of the gags they wanted me to do. At last everything was fine. The bigger the stars the bigger their hearts. They all painstakingly went through the plot of every bit I had to do and by the end of that season I knew the seven gags I've based my whole panto career on!

I was lucky. I've seen beginners given a terrible time by not-so-good jealous comics. Comics who swear the Echo Gag was written by them and that their father invented 'The Tree of Truth'. You'll learn in Paul Harris's marvellous little book that nearly all the panto gags we know and love so well have been handed down to us, like folk music.

They are all here, carefully detailed, with lots of asides and extra little bits of business to keep them fresh. Only a performer could put this collection together in a way that makes them all almost actorproof and Paul, an excellent comedian, has done just that.

This is the book that so many professionals and amateurs have been looking for for years. It will, I predict, become the pantomine bible. Whether you're playing the London Palladium or the village hall my advice is always keep this book – BEHIND YOU!

ROY HUDD
London 1996

THE PROLOGUE

'It's pantomime time'. A magical phrase that conjures up feelings of a typically English Christmas. Dark, frosty nights, the smell of cigars and orange peel, and backstage in the theatre that peculiar odour that pervades every theatre around panto time: a unique mixture of dust, old velvet and rabbit-skin size, a glue-like substance that's used in the preparation of scenery. For many theatres the pantomime season is a saviour. Plays, musicals and television personalities doing one-night stands cannot be relied upon to cover the running costs of the theatre, let alone to make profits. The pantomime season, however, is the time of year when the management can often be guaranteed to make some much-needed money to help ease their way through the following twelve months.

What is it about this form of entertainment that brings people of all ages flocking into the theatre to hear stories that they've heard before, laced with jokes and sketches that they've seen before and to join in singing silly songs that they've sung before? Although the question has been pondered by many people for many years nobody has really come up with a definitive answer; all we know is that it *does* work. Gags that wouldn't raise a smile in any other form of entertainment get guffaws when used in this context. Nobody bats an eyelid when men appear dressed as women, women appear dressed as men and cats, cows and geese start to sing and dance. Ask the theatre-going public why they accept these phenomena and the only answer you're likely to get is, 'Well, it's pantomime isn't it'. A reply that tells us nothing.

Pantomime has been around for many years in one form or another. The first time the word was used about an English entertainment was on 2 March 1717, in an advertisement in *The Daily Courant*, although the production referred to wouldn't be recognizable today as a pantomime. The presentation as we know it stems from about 1860, when music-hall artistes began to be mixed with the actors in these shows. In 1879 Augustus Harris took over the management of the Theatre Royal, Drury Lane and started to pack his productions with music-hall stars. His 1892 production of *Little Bo-Peep, Little Red Riding Hood and Hop o' My Thumb* (they had a penchant for long titles in those days) included Dan Leno, Herbert Campbell, Little Tich and Marie Lloyd in starring roles; all of them were top-of-the-bill music-hall acts.

Although the basic structure of pantomime has stayed the same for over 100 years, certain changes are made from time to time. For example in the 1960s it became fashionable for pop stars to appear in pantomimes, and accordingly we saw the part of the principal boy, traditionally played by a girl, taken over by male singers in many productions. At the time of writing Australian soap actors and sporting personalities seem very much the vogue but the one thing that seems to stay the same year after year are the jokes. People expect to see 'The Ghost Gag' and a splosh scene and are disappointed if they are not included. The fact that they've seen these gags in almost every pantomime they've ever attended makes no difference at all to their amusement; it could even be argued that it enhances their enjoyment of the show. Some of the splosh scenes with the actors getting covered in water, paste and custard pies are very old indeed; they were, in fact, already being presented at the Lincoln's Inn Fields Theatre and at Drury Lane in around 1750. Certainly a lot of the gags and sketches we laugh at today in pantomime first saw the light of day, or to be more correct, the light of the gas lamps, around the turn of the century. Those were the days when the pantomime would contain, perhaps, twenty scenes, a cast of over 100, and would run not for the few weeks we see them today but invariably until Easter.

In 1961 I entered the glittering world of show business by appearing as a young and very green comedian in *Sinbad the Sailor* at the Palace Theatre, Plymouth. The first gag that I was included in by the director was called 'The Drink of Truth', a two-handed gag, which I was to perform with a very talented and luckily for me a very considerate pantomime comedian by the name of Geoff Morris. When I looked in my script there was no mention of 'The Drink of Truth', just the word BIZ where the gag was to go. I was mystified and not a little worried. Was I supposed to know this gag? Was it written down on a separate piece of paper somewhere? How would I learn it? I confided in Geoff Morris. 'Don't worry about it,' he said cheerily, 'we'll talk it through later', and later that day that's just what we did: he explained the gag to me and told me exactly what to say and even how to say it. Nothing was ever written down. The gag was a success and got its laugh whenever we did it. Since then I have performed it in many pantomimes with many different comedians and it's always 'talked through', never written down. The same can be said for most pantomime gags. Originally, I expect they were written in some script somewhere but over the years various comedians and directors have changed a line here and there, added a bit of business and otherwise altered the gag out of all recognition. If you're lucky the script will state 'The Pheasant Gag' or 'The Tree of Truth Gag', or whatever, and at rehearsals the people involved will talk it through, adding or subtracting lines as they go along. Consequently, it is now almost impossible to find these gags in the written form and they are in great danger of being lost. Indeed many gags and bits of 'business' have undoubtedly been lost already.

I have now performed in well over thirty pantomimes and every year, usually around September, all the comics involved in the production get together with the director to discuss the gags to be included in this year's show. It invariably starts with someone naming a gag they would like to do and the director vetoing it because it was done last year. Another gag is named and is dismissed for one reason or another and the next hour is spent trying to think of what other gags there are. Indeed, I have been at production meetings with four or five very experienced comedians where nobody can remember half the gags that exist. A few years ago I was asked to write a pantomime script and was trying to decide which gags were to be used. The obvious ones sprang to mind but I wanted to use some that hadn't been seen quite so often, so I set out to buy a book of pantomime gags. After weeks of searching the bookshelves I still hadn't been able to find what was needed, so I started to research them and write them down. This proved to be far more difficult than I imagined, as everyone has different versions of the same gag and it would be impractical to include all the versions of all the gags. Some have had to be left out because they are purely visual and cannot be translated into the written word. However, I hope I've included all the main ones and some that are new to you.

The authors of the original versions of most of the gags and sketches used in this book will either be very old or no longer with us. I would, however, like to offer them my sincere thanks for all the laughter and fun that their writing has generated over the years. Let us hope it continues to do so for many years to come, for there is no doubt that Christmas wouldn't be the same without the tens of thousands of children and one or two adults who for two-and-a-half hours fall about laughing and shout themselves hoarse at the same gags year after year.

There are over 200 professional pantomimes produced each year in Britain, using about 5000 actors, comedians, singers, dancers and musicians. Add to this the thousands of amateur productions in theatres, church halls, schools, factory canteens and village halls, each one with a cast of up to fifty people, and you have many thousands of people involved with this strange, unexplainable theatrical phenomenon. It is also interesting to note that there are an increasing number of productions, mainly amateur, cropping up in other countries – America, Australia, Canada, and South Africa among them, but wherever you are and whatever you are – actor, singer, comedian, director or just interested party – I hope this compilation will prove not only educational but more importantly entertaining.

A pantomime gag can be anything from a one-line witticism to a ten-minute scene involving several people. Even a look or a funny walk can get a big laugh if placed correctly and, of course, a trip or fall can bring the house down.

One of the funniest falls I've ever seen was in a production of *Dick Whittington*, when I was playing Dame. Heading the bill were that very funny double act Cannon & Ball and they made their first entrance on an old bicycle, Tommy Cannon pedalling with Bobby Ball sitting on the handlebars. They charged on to the stage at great speed and on reaching the front of the stage Tommy pulled on the brakes as hard as possible, shooting Bobby off the handlebars and into the orchestra pit. It got a tremendous laugh every time and Bobby was saved from injury by a pile of mattresses placed in the bottom of the pit.

The following one- or two-line gags can be sprinkled almost anywhere in a production and although they won't get belly laughs they will keep the laughter bubbling along nicely.

A FEW QUICK TITTERS

MAN: My father was a seadog, he seldom came home.
DAME: My father was a dirty dog, he never came home.

DAME: Do you know what love is?
COMIC: Yes. Love is something that starts in Heaven and ends up in the *News of the World*.

COMIC: When I was young I was second to none, well groomed and handsome.
DAME: Now look at you. You're second-hand, not too well and gruesome.

COMIC: May I kiss your hand?
DAME: Why, is my face dirty?

DAME: Every time I'm down in the dumps I buy myself a new hat.
COMIC: I wondered where you got them from.

DAME: I'm wearing a battleship dress.
COMIC: What's a battleship dress?
DAME: Top decks cleared for action.

MAN: If you don't shut up you'll be burnt at the stake or have your
head chopped off.
COMIC: Now what shall I have? Steak or chop?

DAME: That girl will drive me out of my mind.
COMIC: Well you won't have far to go will you?

DAME: I hate you, I hate you, I hate you.
COMIC: Yes and three hates are twenty-four.

MAN: No one can come in here without a ticket.
DAME: My face is my ticket.
MAN: Well I've had orders to punch all tickets.

MAN: You should sprinkle yourself with toilet water.
DAME: I tried that and the seat fell on my head.

DAME: I've had a trying day today.
MAN: Have you really?
DAME: Yes. The butcher tried, the baker tried, the milkman tried . . .

MAN: Madam, I've come for your rent.
DAME: What won the 2.30 at Sandown?
MAN: I'm not interested in what won the 2.30 at Sandown.
DAME: Well you should be, your rent was on it.

DAME: I've worked my fingers to the bone for you and what have I
got to show for it?
COMIC: Boney fingers.

DAME: You haven't been home for three whole days.
COMIC: Three whole days?
DAME: Yes, yesterday, today and tomorrow.

DAME: I want you to go to the butchers and buy a sheep's head. Oh
and ask him to leave the eyes in.

MAN: Leave the eyes in, why?
DAME: Well then it'll see us through the week.

COMIC: How can I tell when this cake's cooked?
DAME: You stick a knife in it and if it comes out clean, it's cooked.
COMIC: Oh good, if it comes out clean I'll stick all the other dirty knives in.

DAME: I've had a pair of knickers made out of a Union Jack.
MAN: Aren't they uncomfortable?
DAME: Well they were until I took the flag-pole out.

DAME: You remind me of the sea.
MAN: Do you mean rough on top but smooth and calm underneath.
DAME: No. You make me sick.

COMIC: You know what happens to people who don't keep their promises, don't you?
DAME: No. What?
COMIC: They become Members of Parliament.

COMIC: I was singing 'Maybe It's Because I'm a Londoner' and I noticed a man crying in the front row. So I said to him 'You must be a Londoner.'
MAN: And what did he say?
COMIC: He said 'No I'm not, I'm a singing teacher.'

COMIC: If brains were gunpowder he wouldn't have enough to blow his hat off.

DAME: I went for a sauna bath the other day. I went into this room all steam and white tiles, took all my clothes off, lay down in the middle of the floor and when the steam cleared I was in a fish and chip shop.

DAME: I want a man who'll pick me up, whirl me round and drain me dry.
COMIC: You don't want a man, you want a spin-drier.

COMIC: She wore a bingo dress.

• 15 •

MAN: What's a bingo dress?
COMIC: Eyes down, look in.

COMIC: I'm just a reckless young blood.
DAME: No you're not, you're a bloodless old wreck.

DAME: I used to be the belle of the ball.
COMIC: Pity you lost your clanger.

DAME: I once had a boyfriend who was so bowlegged I used to hang
him above the door for luck.

COMIC: My pal died from drinking milk.
MAN: How did that happen?
COMIC: The cow fell on him.

DAME: My daddy thinks the world of me.
COMIC: I know. He said he worships the ground that's coming to
you.

DAME: Beauty is only an outer cover.
COMIC: In that case your inner tube's perished.

DAME: I'm going to have my face lifted.
COMIC: When they see what's under it they'll drop it again quick.

DAME: My cooking should be cordon bleu.
COMIC: Your cooking should be cordoned off.

UGLY SISTER 1: If I had a face like yours I'd put it on a wall and
throw a brick at it.
UGLY SISTER 2: Well if I had a face like yours I'd put it on a brick
and throw a wall at it.

UGLY SISTER 1 [*looking in hand mirror*]: Arghhhhhhh. Who's that?
UGLY SISTER 2 [*looking in hand mirror*]: Why, that's me.
UGLY SISTER 1: Thank goodness I thought it was me.

UGLY SISTER 1: Once upon a time I was all pink and dimples.

UGLY SISTER 2: Now look at you, all drink and pimples.

UGLY SISTER 1: I have the complexion of a schoolgirl of sixteen.
UGLY SISTER 2: Well give it back to her then, you're wrinkling it.

UGLY SISTER 1: Oh look, there's two bald-headed men sitting together
   in the audience.
UGLY SISTER 2: No it's not, it's a lady in a low cut dress.

UGLY SISTER 1: We're both very fastidious.
UGLY SISTER 2: Yes, I'm fast and she's hideous.

Lastly in this section, what is possibly the most famous, corny Ugly
Sister gag of all time and believe it or not it still gets a good laugh.

UGLY SISTER 1 [*trying on the slipper*] I can't get my foot in the
   crystal slipper.
UGLY SISTER 2: You couldn't get your foot in the Crystal Palace.

I don't know if any of the gags on the preceding pages would have amused the famous eighteenth-century actor/manager David Garrick but we do know that he didn't like pantomime; he thought it was 'beneath him' and described it as 'a vulgar entertainment'. However by 1750 it was such a popular form of entertainment that Garrick decided that if he wanted to keep his audiences he would have to give them what they wanted and so on Boxing Day he produced his own pantomime called *Queen Mab*. Despite his aversion to this type of presentation it was such a big success that he kept it in his repertoire for twenty-five years.

I have been unable to establish the origin of this next gag so I can't say if David Garrick would have seen it, but I do know it's one that has been around for many years and is a great favourite with pantomime comedians. It's a three-handed gag and is suitable for any subject. It's called . . .

THE NOT HERE GAG

COMIC 1 [*to* COMIC 2]: Would you like a little bet?

COMIC 2: I wouldn't mind. What are we going to bet on?

COMIC 1: I bet you five pounds I can prove you're not here.

COMIC 2: You're mad. Of course I'm here. I saw me arrive. I'll have a fiver on that. [*They both put their money on the floor.*] Go on then, prove I'm not here.

COMIC 1: Right. Now you're not in New York are you?

COMIC 2: No. Of course I'm not in New York.

COMIC 1: And you're not in Paris are you?

COMIC 2: You're right, I'm not in Paris either.

COMIC 1: And you're not in Moscow?

COMIC 2: I'm certainly not in Moscow.

COMIC 1: Well if you're in none of these places you must be somewhere else.

COMIC 2: That's right, I must be somewhere else.

COMIC 1: And if you're somewhere else, you can't be here.

[COMIC 1 *picks up the money and exits laughing.*]

COMIC 2: What a swindle. I'll have to try that on someone else to get my money back.

[*Enter* COMIC 3.]

COMIC 3: Hello. What are you up to?

COMIC 2: I've just been thinking of a brilliant way to make money. Do you want to have a go?

COMIC 3: Yes. I always like to make money. What do I do?

COMIC 2: Well, I bet you ten pounds I can prove you're not here.

COMIC 3: You're off your trolley. Go on then, brains, go ahead and prove it. Here's my money.

[*They both put their money down.*]

COMIC 2: Right. Now you're not in Scunthorpe are you?

COMIC 3: No, I'm not in Scunthorpe.

COMIC 2: And you're not in Dymchurch are you?

COMIC 3: I'm pretty sure I'm not in Dymchurch.

COMIC 2: And you're not in Littlehampton are you?

COMIC 3: No, I've never been to Littlehampton.

COMIC 2: Well if you're in none of these places you must be somewhere else.

COMIC 3: Well of course I must.

COMIC 2: And if you're somewhere else you're not here.

[COMIC 2 *picks up the money and exits.*]

COMIC 3: I think I've just been bamboozled out of my money. I'll have to try to get it back.

[COMIC 1 *enters.*]

COMIC 1: What are you doing stood standing here, waiting for a cup of tea?

COMIC 3: No, I'm waiting for a mug.

COMIC 1: Well you won't get one of them here.

COMIC 3: Oh I don't know, I think I'm just about to. Would you like to earn me some money? I mean would you like to win some money?

COMIC 1 [*gives knowing look to audience*]: I wouldn't mind having a go. What do I do?

COMIC 3: Well I bet you twenty pounds that I can prove that you're not all here.

COMIC 1 [*to audience*]: Have you ever had a feeling that you've been somewhere before? Go on then, prove I'm not here.

[*They both put their money down.*]

COMIC 3: Right now, you're not in, er . . . you're not in Scunchurch are you?

COMIC 1: No. I'm not in Scunchurch.

COMIC 3: And neither are you in Dymthorpe are you?

COMIC 1: I am definitely not in Dymthorpe.

COMIC 3: And you're not in Hampton Wick are you?

COMIC 1: I am not in Hampton Wick, no.

COMIC 3: Well if you're in none of these places you must be somewhere else.

COMIC 1: Well of course I must.

COMIC 3: And if you're somewhere else, you're not here.

COMIC 1: You're right.

[COMIC 1 *picks up all the money and starts to exit.*]

COMIC 3: Hey that's my money. I've just won that. You've pinched my money.

COMIC 1: Don't be daft. How could I have pinched your money. I'm not here.

[COMIC 1 *runs off chased by* COMIC 3.]

The 1970–71 pantomime season was a memorable one for me. I was playing Ugly Sister in *Cinderella* at the Opera House, Belfast. There was a lot of trouble going on in Northern Ireland, security was very tight around the town and people were understandably jumpy. One night during the performance my 'Sister' and I rushed from the stage to our dressing-room to execute a very quick change of costume. As we pushed the dressing-room door open and started to run into the room the window to the street exploded as something came flying towards us. I stepped back out of the room, knocking over my 'Sister' who in turn knocked into a line of chorus dancers trying to run up the passage to their room, half of whom fell into a heap in the corridor. Luckily our room was next to the stage door and seeing what had happened the doorkeeper rushed into the street and caught two little boys trying to run away from the scene of the crime. Meanwhile, I was lying on top of my 'Sister' and half a dozen assorted chorus girls waiting for the inevitable explosion, convinced that a bomb had been thrown through the window. When questioned, the two culprits admitted they had thrown a brick through the window because we wouldn't let Cinderella go to the ball. It was pure coincidence that they had picked the right window. Throughout all the commotion and noise that this incident had generated, poor Buttons and Cinderella had been trying to perform the following gag. It's called 'The Y Dance' and has been around as long as the common cold and some would say it's about as funny; however, it seems to work best when played by sympathetic characters like Buttons and Cinderella. Here's my version:

THE Y DANCE

BUTTONS: Hey Cinders, do you know the Y dance?
CINDERS: No, I don't think I've ever heard of that dance, Buttons.
BUTTONS: Would you like me to teach it to you?
CINDERS: Oh yes please, Buttons.
BUTTONS: Well first of all you stand close to me like this. [*They stand face to face with their noses about two inches apart.*] Then you put your left arm round here. [*He takes her left arm and puts it around his waist.*]
CINDERS: Is this right, Buttons?

BUTTONS: Oh yes. That's ever so right, Cinders.

CINDERS: You are showing me the Y dance aren't you Buttons?

BUTTONS: Well of course I'm showing you the Y dance.

CINDERS: Well what do I do now?

BUTTONS: You take your right arm and you put it round here. [*He takes her right arm and puts it round his waist.*] Then I take my right arm and put it here. [*He puts his arm around her waist.*] Then I put my left arm here. [*He puts his left arm around her waist.*]

CINDERS: What do we do now?

BUTTONS: You put your cheek next to my cheek.

[*They do so.* BUTTONS *is panting by now.*]

And now . . .

CINDERS: And now Buttons?

BUTTONS: Why dance?

I played Ugly Sister in another production of *Cinderella*, this time at the Theatre Royal in Newcastle. David Jason played Buttons in this, the only pantomime he has ever agreed to appear in. He was perfect in the part of Buttons but not so perfect in one of the gags he was to do. He was supposed to build a flying machine and fly across the stage in it to impress Cinderella, the flying to be carried out by means of a harness and 'invisible' wire. At the first dress rehearsal he was put into the harness, which is worn under the costume. Now some of these harnesses have a nasty habit of cutting into you where you'd rather not be cut into and David had one of these. He was hoisted into the air with this little flying machine fixed round his waist and a look of pure agony on his face. The wire was activated and he flew across the stage at great speed and crashed into the scenery on the other side. The set wobbled dangerously and threatened to fall on poor Cinderella and David was left dangling in mid-air, strung up like an oven-ready chicken while all the stage hands rushed to hold up the scenery.

Needless to say this gag was cut out of the script there and then and as far as I know David has never 'flown' on stage since.

He did though perform the following gag beautifully and without mishap. The kissing gag is a silly little gag but quite endearing.

THE KISS

BUTTONS: Cinders, would you like a little bet with me?

CINDERS: What sort of a bet, Buttons?

BUTTONS: Well, I bet you fifty pence that I can kiss you on the lips without touching you.

CINDERS: Oh Buttons, that's silly, how can you do that?

BUTTONS: You bet me the fifty pence and I'll show you how it's done.

CINDERS: Kiss me on the lips without touching me?

BUTTONS: Yes. Go on then, bet.

CINDERS: All right then, I bet.

BUTTONS: Close your eyes. [*She closes her eyes and he kisses her full on the lips, then falls flat on his back.*]

CINDERS: But you did touch me, Buttons.

BUTTONS [*getting up*]: Yes I know. Here's your fifty pence but boy, was it worth it!

    [*She chases him off.*]

Throughout the years betting gags have always been very popular in pantomime and there have been many variations on the theme. I researched the following one to try to find when it was first used but as so often happens I could only establish that it has been around for many years. I have heard it called the 'Sweaty Socks Gag' but a far more savoury title is its original one, which is . . .

STICKS

FEED 1 [*to* COMIC]: I bet you a fiver you can't answer everything I say with the same word.

COMIC: What do you mean, answer everything you say with the same word?

FEED 1: Well, whatever I ask you, you must answer sticks.

COMIC: That's a daft answer isn't it, sticks?

FEED 1: That's what you've got to say if you want to win.

COMIC: I see. So if I say sticks to everything you ask, I'll win a fiver?

FEED 1: That's right. Now put your money down.

COMIC: I've got to put a fiver down, have I?

FEED 1: Yes you have. Come on. Put it down.

[*They both put a five pound note on the floor.*] Now are you ready?

COMIC: Yes, I'm ready.

FEED 1 [*picking up the two fivers*]: That's a fiver I've won.

COMIC: What do you mean?

FEED 1: You didn't say sticks.

COMIC: That's not fair. I didn't realize we'd started. Can I have another go?

FEED 1: Go on then, put down another fiver.

[*They both put down another five pound note each.*] Now, are you ready this time?

COMIC: Sticks.

FEED 1: I didn't get you that time did I?

COMIC: No you didn't. [FEED *picks up the two notes.*] What are you doing?

FEED 1: You didn't say sticks.

COMIC: Oh no, I've done it again. Let me have one more go.

FEED 1: All right then. One more go. Put your money down. [*They both put their money down.*] Are you ready?

COMIC: Sticks.

FEED 1: I didn't get you that time did I?

COMIC: Sticks.

FEED 1: You're getting very good at this aren't you?

COMIC: Sticks.

FEED 1: What would you rather have, the money or the sticks.

COMIC: Sticks.

FEED 1: Right then, I'll have the money.

[*He exits with the money.*]

COMIC: Oh no, I've been caught again. I'll have to try to get some of my money back. Oh look, here comes someone, I'll try it on him. [*Enter* FEED 2.] I say, would you like to earn a fiver?

FEED 2: That all depends what I have to do for it. I can't work, I've got trouble with my back.

COMIC: What sort of trouble?

FEED 2: I have trouble getting it off the bed in the morning.

COMIC: This is easy. All you have to do is say sticks to everything I ask you.

FEED 2: Everything you ask me I must answer sticks?

COMIC: That's right and I bet you a fiver you can't do it.

FEED 2 [*to audience*]: He's a couple of sandwiches short of a picnic. Of course I can do it.

COMIC: Well put your money down then.

FEED 2: Right. Here's my fiver. [*Puts five pound note on floor.*]

COMIC: And here's mine. [*He puts his money down. To audience.*] Right, this is where I earn some money back. Are you ready?

FEED 2: Sticks.

COMIC: I didn't get you that time did I?

FEED 2: Sticks.

COMIC: Er. What did you have for your breakfast this morning?

FEED 2: Sticks.

COMIC: What did you get for Christmas this year?

FEED 2: Sticks.

COMIC [*beginning to get desperate*]: What do you put in the pan to make a lovely stew?

FEED 2: Sticks.

COMIC [*very desperate*]: I know, I know, what would you rather have, the money or the sticks?

FEED 2: The money. [*He picks up the money and goes to exit.*]
COMIC: You're not supposed to say that.
FEED 2: Oh yes I am, I've heard it before. [*Exit.*]

Red Riding Hood is a pantomime subject that has been around for many years. It first appeared as a pantomime in 1803 and was written by Charles Dibdin Junior, who was at the time manager of the Sadler's Wells Theatre in London. He was also the man who gave the great Grimaldi his first job as a clown on Easter Monday 1800 at the same theatre, and Grimaldi spent every summer of his career appearing at Sadler's Wells except for one, the summer of 1817, when because of a disagreement with the management he wasn't engaged. The public were incensed at his non-appearance and showed their displeasure by staying away in their thousands and at the end of that summer the theatre had lost over £2,500!

Many years ago I appeared in a very tatty production of *Red Riding Hood*, in a theatre at Ramsgate, which I don't think took £2,500 the whole season, so bad was it. The wolf's skin looked like an old army blanket badly sewn together, and at one performance, as the wolf swaggered on stage for his first entrance proclaiming 'I am the wicked wolf from the depths of the forest,' a little boy in the circle shouted out 'Fuck off Fido' and the Big Bad Wolf ran off the stage in tears. One of the few good things about this production was the gag I reproduce below. It requires the use of an inner tube from a tractor and a car tyre. It's a good gag but the whole thing does rely on having a really large tractor inner tube for the tag.

THE TYRE GAG

[FEED *and* COMIC *enter from opposite sides and meet.* FEED *has a car tyre in his hand.*]

COMIC: What are you doing walking around with that old tyre, all worn out and tatty?

FEED: Worn out and tatty. This tyre's not worn out and tatty.

COMIC: I wasn't referring to the tyre.

FEED: This is a magic tyre.

COMIC: A magic tyre? Tyres can't be magic. What's it do, roll down the road and turn into a garage?

FEED: No, no, no.

COMIC: No, no, no.

FEED: No. This tyre is magic because it can go all the way around the town by itself.

COMIC: By itself? You mean without being fixed to a car?

FEED:: Without being fixed to a car.

COMIC: Without a map?

FEED: Without a map.

COMIC: How does it find its way around this town without a map?

FEED: Because it's magic, that's why.

COMIC: I'd like to see it do that.

FEED: Would you like to see it do that?

COMIC: That's what I've just said.

FEED: Very well. I shall make it go all the way around the town and come back here.

COMIC: This I have got to see. Come on, get it started.

FEED: Watch closely.

COMIC: I'm watching closely.

> [FEED *pushes the tyre off stage left and describes its journey around town using local street names.*]

FEED: There it goes. Down the corridor, out of the stage door and into the street. It turns left at the end of the street into the High Street, down the High Street past Woolworths, past the Post Office and up the alley by the side of the greengrocers. Down the hill to the park gates, through the park, out the other gate and along the tow path by the river. It turns left by the war memorial, through the children's playground and back into the High Street; it's turning right into this road, turns into the stage door, along the corridor and here it comes now. [*The tyre rolls on from stage right and is picked up by the* COMIC.]

> [*This description of the tyre's journey must be spoken at a fast pace rather like a radio commentator describing a horse race. It is more effective if the journey described is a recognizable journey around the town the show is playing in.*]

COMIC: That was very good, but, it's strange you showing me a magic tyre.

FEED: Why is it strange?

COMIC: It is strange because I've got a magic tyre as well. I'll go and get it.

> [COMIC *walks to the side of the stage with the tyre. He holds the tyre off stage out of sight and talks to a stage-hand.*]
> Will you take this tyre off me and hand me my magic tyre? Thank you kind sir.

[*He immediately brings the same tyre back into view.*]

[*To audience, who obviously realize that it is the same tyre.*] Oh no it isn't.

AUDIENCE: Oh yes it is.

COMIC: Oh no it isn't.

AUDIENCE: Oh yes it is.

COMIC: It isn't. It just looks similar because it was made at the same factory. On the same shift. By the brother-in-law of the man who made the other one.

FEED: Well come on then, set it off.

COMIC: Right, here it goes. [*He rolls the tyre off stage left.*] There it goes down the corridor out of the stage door and it's stopped.

FEED: Why has it stopped?

COMIC: It's thinking which is the quickest way to go. It's off again, up the road into the High Street, along the High Street through the front door of Woolworths, out the back door, round by McDonalds and it's stopped.

FEED: Why has it stopped by McDonalds?

COMIC: It's eating some chicken nuggets.

FEED: Is it happy now?

COMIC: Yes but the chicken's not very pleased. It's off again, through the park out the other side and it's stopped again.

FEED: Why has it stopped this time?

COMIC: It's tired. It's off. Round by the war memorial, through the children's playground and it's stopped again.

FEED: Not again. What's it stopped this time for?

COMIC: It's stopped for an ice-cream.

FEED: How can a car tyre eat an ice-cream?

COMIC: It licks it.

FEED: It's going to be a very overweight tyre at this rate.

COMIC: Don't worry, it's on a high fibre diet.

FEED: It'll be full of wind.

COMIC: Well it saves you blowing it up. Here it comes now. Down the road, into the stage door, up the stairs into the circle, along the back of the circle, down the stairs, along the corridor, into the wings and here it comes now.

[*He indicates stage left and a very large tractor inner tube is rolled on stage right and hits them in the back. As they both fall over there is a black-out.*]

This next gag is a quick laugh and is also the first gag I ever performed on a professional stage. It was at the Palace Theatre, Plymouth, in the pantomime *Sinbad the Sailor*. This subject is seldom seen these days and neither is the gag. I can't think why as it's a good old panto quickie.

THE DRINK OF TRUTH

COMIC: I have here in this bottle a very special drink.

FEED: You don't mean a Guinness shandy.

COMIC: No. This is even more special than a Guinness shandy. It's called the drink of truth.

FEED: The drink of truth?

COMIC: Yes. One drink from this bottle and you can't help but tell the truth.

FEED: You mean if I have a drink of that I cannot tell a lie?

COMIC: That's right. As supplied to the House of Commons bar.

FEED: One little sip and I tell the truth.

COMIC: One gulp and you're gullible.

FEED: I must have a go of that. [*He takes the bottle and drinks. He immediately spits it out and there is a stage flash.*] That's petrol.

COMIC: That's the truth.

[COMIC *is chased off by the* FEED.]

NOTE: When I first performed this gag I was a very inexperienced performer and one night I forgot to take the prop bottle on with me and decided I would have to cut the gag out. When we got off stage the very irate comedian I was to perform the gag with asked me why I had cut it out. 'I forgot the bottle,' I stammered. 'And we can't do the gag without the bottle'. 'This is pantomime, laddie,' he stormed. 'All you had to say was, I have a very special drink here, in this invisible bottle and we could have performed the gag. Don't ever cut a laugh, laddie.' My first lesson was learned.

'A Little Bit of Heaven' is the title of an old song and also the title of the next gag. The first few words of the song are the pivot for the gag but don't worry if you don't know the tune; it really doesn't matter.

The gag centres around a full sack coming down from the flies on a wire and hitting the singer on the head. Care should be taken with the sack, however, otherwise the singer could get a bigger surprise than he bargained for. In the early stages of my career I took part in this gag in a touring production of *Cinderella*, it was not a happy event! After a week on the road, Prince Charming was sacked for going on stage drunk and throwing up in the ballroom scene. The comedian playing Buttons had a stand-up fight in the wings with one of the Ugly Sisters, and poor Cinderella, who was played by an actress who was thirty years too old for the part, fell down the stairs, having had a gin too many and damaged her leg, which resulted in the said leg blowing up to the size of a somewhat mature tree trunk complete with knobbly bits. This elderly Princess spent the rest of the season limping around the stage with one fat leg and one thin leg. Is it any wonder that Prince Charming threw up in the ballroom scene? Amidst all this chaos a stage-hand who was charged with the job of preparing the sack for the following gag nearly killed the actor playing the Baron. He filled the sack with crumpled-up newspaper, tied on the wire and pulled it up to the flies out of sight of the audience. That night when we came to do the gag he released the wire on cue but the weight of the paper-filled sack was not enough to propel it downwards and on to the head of the Baron, who was the first person to try singing the song. As the sack refused to put in an appearance, we had to abandon the gag and the stage-hand was hauled over the coals by the producer and told to make the sack heavier for the next performance. Unfortunately for the Baron the stage-hand put a stage weight into the sack. These weigh about twenty pounds each and are used for holding the scenery braces down. That night the Baron started to sing the song, the wire holding up the sack was released and it hurtled towards the unsuspecting Baron's head. Once again we had to abandon the gag and this time also drag off stage the prostrate body of the Baron. He was an actor in his late seventies and when we saw him lying in a pool of blood we all thought the worst, but luckily this actor was a tough old bird and survived to act another day. Whether he attempted this gag again is not recorded but it is worth including in a pantomime as it does get big laughs.

A LITTLE BIT OF HEAVEN

COMIC [*to audience*]: I've just been told that there is a magic spot on this floor and if I can find it and then stand on it and sing a certain song, I'll get a present. So I'm going to look for it. [*He wanders around the stage looking for the cross marked on the floor.*] Here it is, I've found it. Now I've got to stand on it and sing an old song called 'A Little Bit of Heaven'. I only know the first line, I hope that will do. [*Sings.*] A little bit of heaven fell from out the sky one day. [*On the word 'fell' a weighted sack on a line descends and hits him on the head, then goes back from where it came.*] Hey, that's not a very nice present. Somebody's mucking about with me. I know, I'll try it on somebody else. [*Enter* FEED.]

FEED: What are you doing hanging around here?

COMIC: It's funny you should ask that. I've found a magic cross on the floor.

FEED: A magic cross. What do you mean?

COMIC: Well if you stand on this magic cross and sing 'A Little Bit of Heaven', you'll get a present.

FEED: Really. I must have a go at that.

COMIC: Shall we let him have a go, boys and girls?

[*Audience all shout.*] All right then, this is the magic spot, come and stand on it.

    [*He does so.*]

FEED: Is this right?

COMIC: Oh that's perfect. Now, when I say go you must start to sing. Go.

    [*The* FEED *starts to sing the song, the sack descends and hits him and the* COMIC *exits laughing.*]

FEED [*Rubbing his head*]: Oh that wasn't a very nice present. I know what I'll do, I'll get my own back on the next person that comes along.

    [*Enter* DAME.]

DAME: Oh look. A man standing by himself. I'll go and stand next to him and see if he likes manure girls. I mean mature girls.

[*She stands right next to him.*] Would you like a date with a young lady who has a figure like an egg-timer?

FEED: Why? Do you know of one?

DAME: I've got a figure like an egg-timer.

FEED: Yes but all your sand's gone to the bottom.

DAME: Cheek.

FEED: Never mind Sarah, would you like a nice big present?

DAME: Don't be personal, young man. I'm a lady. If I wasn't such a lady I'd give you a kick in the gob.

FEED: You don't understand. There is a magic cross here and if you stand on it and sing 'A Little Bit of Heaven', you'll get a present.

DAME: I haven't had a present for a long time. I'd love to have a go.

FEED: Well here's the spot. Come and stand on it and sing the song and you'll get your present.

DAME: Very well then. I hope you realize I sing like a bird.

FEED: I know you do. A pelican with a bill full of fish.

DAME: I shall ignore that remark and sing.

[*She sings. The sack comes down and hits her. The* FEED *staggers off laughing.*]

Well, what a cheek. I've never been so insulated in all my life.

[*Enter* COMIC.]

COMIC: What are you rambling on about?

DAME: I'm not rambling, I'm raving.

COMIC: I always thought you were raving. What are you raving about?

DAME: I er . . . I was er . . . I was raving about what a lovely day it is.

COMIC [*with a wink to the audience*]: Lovely day. It looks to me as if the heavens are about to fall in.

DAME: What do you know about it . . . I mean . . . er . . . I'm glad you're here because I want you to do me a favour.

COMIC: I bet you say that to all the boys.

DAME: No really. There's a magic cross here.

COMIC: I see.

DAME: Yes and if you stand on it and sing 'A Little Bit of Heaven' you'll get a surprise.

COMIC [*to audience*]: So will she.

DAME: What did you say?

COMIC: I said it's nearly time for tea. Now, where is this cross?

DAME: It's right here. [*The* COMIC *stands on it.*]

COMIC: And I just have to sing?

DAME: That's right, you just sing and you'll get it.

COMIC: Right, here I go. [*Sings.*] A little bit of heaven fell from out the sky one day.

• *34* •

[*On the word 'fell' he takes a step forward and the sack goes behind him.*]

DAME: No, no, no, you mustn't move forward. Just stand on the cross and sing it.

COMIC: You mean just stand on this cross, the one that's under my feet, and then sing?

DAME: That's what I said, didn't I?

COMIC: OK. I'll do it again. [*Sings.*] A little bit of heaven fell from out the sky one day. [*This time on the word 'fell' he takes a step backwards and the sack goes in front of him.*]

DAME [*getting exasperated*]: No, no, no, you don't take a step backward, you don't take a step forward, you just take a step stood still and stand on the spot and blooming well sing with your mouth.

COMIC: I'm sorry. I'll have another bash. [*He sings again and this time on the word 'fell' he takes a step sideways and once again the sack misses. The* DAME *is now at her wits' end and is shouting at the* COMIC *as she shows him what to do.*]

DAME: You stupid excuse for an idiot. You don't walk forwards, you don't walk backwards, you don't walk sidewards and you don't walk up in the air. You just stand still on this spot, like this, and you sing.

[*Sings.*] A little bit of heaven fell . . .

[*The sack crashes down on her head and knocks her over.*]

COMIC [*calmly*]: Well why didn't you say? [*He walks over and stands on the spot and sings. This time when he gets to the word 'fell' the sack does not come down. A second line comes down beside him, on the end of which is a basket containing a bottle of whiskey. He takes the bottle out of the basket.*] Well, thank you very much. How kind you are.

[*He exits, leaving the* DAME *tearing her hair out.*]

'The Tree of Truth' is a two-handed gag that was first performed in pantomime by Dan Leno and Herbert Campbell at the Theatre Royal, Drury Lane, at the turn of the century. Dan Leno was a small wiry man, Herbert Campbell was the opposite, over six feet tall and weighing over twenty stone. They must have looked terribly funny, one as Dame, the other as Comic, sitting under the tree which dropped acorns on their head whenever they told a lie. This sketch is almost certainly originally written by J. Hickory Wood, who started to write pantomimes as we know them today. He got rid of the idea of the cast all speaking in rhyming couplets, except for the immortals, and ceased to include the Harlequinade, which had dominated pantomimes until then. Whenever I have seen this sketch performed, the acorns which fell on Leno and Campbell have been replaced by either grapefruit or oranges. I don't know if this is because they are easier to see or if it's simply a case of inflation. Either way it's a sketch that is well worth including in this book.

THE TREE OF TRUTH

[*Enter* COMIC *and* DAME.]

COMIC: I'm really tired, I've been up all day breathing. I must have a little sit down.

[*Sits on bench under the tree.*]

DAME: Yes I'm really tired as well. [*Sits next to* COMIC.] I've been up since six o'clock this morning working hard. [*Grapefruit falls on her head.*]

Ow, what was that?

COMIC: That was a grapefruit. You are sitting under the tree of truth.

DAME: The tree of truth. That's a daft name for a tree. What does it mean?

COMIC: It means that everytime you tell a fib a grapefruit will fall from this tree and hit you on the head.

DAME: Well that won't bother me because I don't tell fibs. [*A grapefruit falls on her head.*] Ow.

COMIC: There you are, just as I said, a grapefruit fell on your head. You must have told a lie.

DAME: No I didn't. [*Another grapefruit falls on her head.*]

COMIC: You must have told another one then.

DAME: It must be a bit deaf. It's not hearing me properly. I've never done anything naughty in my life. [*Another grapefruit falls on her head.*]

COMIC: You're a bigger fibber than I am.

DAME: I don't like this tree very much. I think we should swap places. [*They change places on the bench.*]

COMIC: Does that suit you now?

DAME: That's much better. Now tell me, do you like my new hair-do?

COMIC: Oh yes I think it's lovely. [*A Grapefruit falls on his head.*]

DAME: What was that?

COMIC: Oh don't worry, I think it was just a loose one. The wind must have blown it down.

DAME: As I was saying. What do you really think of my new hairstyle?

COMIC: Well, I think it's very . . . [*Grapefruit on a line starts to descend slowly*] . . . different [*the grapefruit goes up*] and it suits . . . [*It starts to descend again*] it suits . . . some people. [*It goes up again.*]

DAME: Yes, but does it make me look attractive?

COMIC: Oh, it makes you look very . . . [*Grapefruit starts to descend*] . . . thingy. [*grapefruit goes up.*]

DAME: Do you mean it enhances my natural beauty?

COMIC: Oh yes . . . [*Grapefruit starts to descend*] . . . it . . . er . . . it . . . it makes use of what you've got. [*Grapefruit goes back.*]

DAME: Do you know, I really think you're after me, aren't you?

COMIC: What makes you think that?

DAME: All these flattering compliments you keep giving me, with your mouth. Come on admit it, you're after my charms aren't you?

COMIC: I didn't even know you had a charm bracelet.

DAME: Come along, be honest, you are after me aren't you?

COMIC: I . . . er . . . I think . . . I . . . [*Grapefruit starts to descend*]. Or maybe I'm . . . [*Grapefruit goes up*].

DAME: Well come along, give me an answer.

COMIC: I'm overcome with emulsion, I mean emotion. The sight of your face has stunned me into silence. I can't answer.

DAME: Oh how touching. It's so nice to meet a man who is completely honest.

[*A great big pile of grapefruit falls on to the* COMIC's *head. He runs off chased by the* DAME.]

Henry Fielding, the novelist, had several goes at writing pantomimes. The first, in 1736, was called *Tumble-Down Dick or Phaeton in the Suds*. He described it as 'A Dramatick Entertainment of Walking, in Serious and Foolish Characters, Interlarded with Burlesque, Grotesque, Comick Interludes, call'd Harlequin a Pick-Pocket'. Not quite the way you'd describe a modern day production. I don't for a minute think this next gag would have been in it but you never know: anything can happen in pantomime.

THE ECHO GAG

[*Enter* COMIC *and* FEED.]

COMIC: Do you know, I'm so broke that if ten pound notes were on sale at Woolworths for fifty pence each, I wouldn't be able to buy any.

FEED: Well in that case you'll be interested in my new idea for making money.

COMIC: You've got an idea for making money?

FEED: And it's suited to you.

COMIC: I'm all ears.

FEED: I know, but we can't all be perfect.

COMIC: Never mind the cheek, how can I make some money?

FEED: I'll explain it to you. First of all did you know there is an echo here.

COMIC: Do what?

FEED: Did you know there's an echo here?

COMIC: Here I say, there's an echo here.

FEED: No that's me.

COMIC: Do what?

FEED: No that's me.

COMIC: There it is again.

FEED: No. Listen to me. There is no echo here.

COMIC: But you just said there was.

FEED: I know I said there was but there isn't.

COMIC: There isn't?

FEED: There isn't.

COMIC: There it is again.

FEED: There is no echo here but we tell people there is.

COMIC [*to audience*]: There might not be an echo here but there's certainly an idiot and I'm standing next to him. [*To* FEED.] What are you talking about?

FEED: We will pretend there is an echo here to make money out of people. It's simple.

COMIC: I think you're the one that's simple. How can we make money by pretending there's an echo here?

FEED: I'll show you. Just stand over there, out of sight and repeat everything I say.

COMIC: I repeat everything you say?

FEED: Yes. Now get out of sight. [COMIC *goes off stage.*] Can you hear me?

COMIC [*entering*]: Yes, of course I can.

FEED: You're not supposed to come out here. Keep out of sight and repeat everything I say.

COMIC: I'm sorry. I didn't realize. [*He exits.*]

FEED: Can you hear me?

COMIC: Can you hear me?

FEED: How are you?

COMIC [*entering*]: I've got a bit of trouble with my back . . .

FEED: No, no, no. You stay out of sight and repeat everything I say.

COMIC: I'm sorry. I've got it now. I'll be all right. [*He exits.*]

FEED: Hello.

COMIC: Hello.

FEED: How are you?

COMIC: How are you?

FEED: My dog has fleas.

COMIC [*entering*]: You want to put some powder on it, that'll get rid of them.

FEED: No, no, no. Will you do as I say? [*He looks off.*] There's somebody coming. Quick, get out of sight and remember what I said.

COMIC: All right. All right, don't worry. I'll be brilliant.

FEED: That'll make a change.

[COMIC *exits. Enter* DAME *from opposite side.*]

DAME: Hello. How are you?

FEED: I'm very well but I'm a bit worried about this echo here.

DAME: What echo where?

FEED: This echo here.

DAME: What are you talking about, there's no echo here.

FEED: Oh yes there is. A big loud echo.

DAME: Don't be silly, I know this place well. There's no echo here. I used to do my courting here, if there was an echo I'd have had twice as much fun.

FEED: Well I'll bet you ten pounds there is an echo here.

DAME: I'll take you up on that. Come along prove it.

FEED: Right. Listen to this. Hello.

COMIC: Hello.

FEED: How are you?

COMIC: How are you?

FEED: Oompa, oompa.

COMIC: Stick it up your jumper.

DAME: That's very good but can I try it out?

FEED: Yes of course you can.

DAME: Hello.

COMIC: Hello.

DAME: I am here.

COMIC: I am here.

DAME: I am ready for you.

COMIC: I am ready for you.

DAME: Come and get me.

COMIC: You must be joking.

DAME: Would you like to drink champagne from my slipper?

COMIC: Would you like a slap in the face with a kipper.

DAME: I know where.

COMIC: I know where.

DAME: You can get.

COMIC: You can get.

DAME: A bottle of whiskey.

COMIC: A bottle of whiskey.

DAME: For fifty pence.

COMIC [*running on to* DAME]: Where's that then . . .

    [FEED *and* DAME *chase him off.*]

There are certain gags that really baffle the audience as they actually seem to work out in a perverse sort of way. These gags usually involve either borrowing or lending money and are great personal favourites of mine. The following one has been known by various titles, 'The Money Gag', 'The Two Pound Gag', 'The Borrowing Gag' but I've always called it by the tag line which is:

NOW WE'RE ALL SQUARE

[*The* FEED *is already on stage when the* COMIC *enters.*]

FEED: Ah, I'm glad you've come along.

COMIC: Why? What do you want?

FEED: Remember that two pounds I loaned you?

COMIC: Yes I remember it well. I spent it on some sweets.

FEED: Well I need it back. Can I have it please?

COMIC: I haven't got any money at the moment. Wait a minute though, I might be able to help. [*To musical director.*] Can you lend me two pounds please?

M.D. I haven't got two pounds but I'll lend you a pound. [*He hands* COMIC *a pound.*]

COMIC: Thanks very much. That'll help. [*To* FEED.] Now, I owe you two pounds; here's a pound of it and I still owe you a pound.

   [*Hands pound to* FEED *and exits.*]

FEED: Thank you very much.

   [*Enter* DAME.]

DAME: I'm glad I've caught you. You owe me two pounds and I need it. Can you pay me?

FEED: Well I haven't got two pounds but here is a pound and I'll still owe you a pound.

   [*He hands her a pound and exits.*]

DAME: Thank you. At least I can get some shopping.

   [*Enter* COMIC.]

COMIC: Ah there you are. I want you.

DAME: What's the matter?

COMIC: You owe me two pounds and I need it.

DAME: I've only got a pound. You can have that and I'll still owe you a pound.

[*She hands him a pound.*]

COMIC: Well thank you, that's something.

[*Enter* FEED.] I'm glad you've come back, I owe you a pound don't I?

FEED: Yes you do.

COMIC: Well there it is. [*Hands him a pound.*] That's you and I square.

FEED: [*To* DAME.] I owe you a pound don't I?

DAME: You certainly do.

FEED: Well here it is. [*He hands over the pound.* That's you and I square.

DAME [*to* COMIC]: I owe you a pound, don't I?

COMIC: I'm sure you do.

DAME: Well here it is then. [*Hands the pound over.*] That's you and I square.

COMIC [*to Musical Director*]: Remember that pound I borrowed off you?

M.D. Yes I do.

COMIC: Here it is. [*Hands it over.*]

ALL: Now we're all square.

[*Exeunt.*]

This is another daft little money gag that must have been performed by hundreds of comics over the years but has gradually been lost from most scripts. I have only ever used this gag once, in a production of *Aladdin* at Southend in the 1970s, and have never seen it performed in any other production. It used to be called 'The Three Pound Gag', but owing to inflation I've made it a bit more valuable and called it:

THE FIFTEEN POUND GAG

[DAME *is on stage looking suitably downcast.* COMIC *enters.*]

COMIC: Hello. You look fed up. What's the matter?

DAME: I'm depressed.

COMIC: Well whenever I'm depressed I go out and treat myself. Why don't you go out and buy yourself something.

DAME: What a good idea. I'll go down to Mark's and Spender's and buy myself a bicycle. [*They both start to exit in opposite directions.*] Oh I've just remembered, I haven't got any money.

COMIC: That's all right. I've got fifteen pounds. You can borrow that. Here you are, three fivers, one two three. [*Counts them into her hand.*]

DAME: Thank you very much. That's fifteen pounds I owe you. [*Both start to exit.*]

COMIC: Oh. Hold on. Now I've lent you all my money I've none left for myself.

DAME: That's all right, I'll lend you a fiver. There you are. [*Hands him a fiver.*]

COMIC: Thank you very much.

DAME: So that's ten pounds I owe you and five pounds you owe me. Right?

COMIC [*doubtfully*]: Right.

DAME: So if I give you the ten pounds I owe you [*she gives him back two fivers*] and you give me the fiver you owe me. [*Takes back a fiver.*] Now we're straight, right?

[*She starts to exit.*]

COMIC: Just a minute.

DAME: What's the matter?

COMIC: That's not right.

DAME: You don't quite understand do you? Now look, I'll be you and you be me. [*They change sides.* DAME *takes the three fivers.*] Now ask me to lend you fifteen pounds.

COMIC: Please will you lend me fifteen pounds?

DAME: Certainly. Five, ten, fifteen. [*Counts the notes into his hands.*] Now that's fifteen pounds you owe me.

COMIC: Thank you. [*Both start to exit.*]

DAME: Just a minute. Now that I've lent you all my money I've none left for myself.

COMIC: That's all right. I'll lend you a fiver.

   [*Gives her a fiver.*]

DAME: Thank you. So now I owe you a fiver and you owe me ten pounds, right.

COMIC [*doubtfully*]: Right.

DAME: So if I give you the fiver I owe you [*hands him a fiver*] and you give me the ten pounds you owe me, [*takes two fivers off him*] now we're straight.

   [*Starts to exit.*]

COMIC: No we're not.

DAME: You know what's the matter don't you? You're on the wrong side. [*They change sides.* DAME *takes the three fivers.*]

   Now ask me to lend you fifteen pounds.

COMIC: Please will you lend me fifteen pounds?

DAME: Certainly my boy. [*Counts the notes into his hands.*] Five, ten, fifteen. Now that's fifteen pounds you owe me, right?

COMIC: Right.

DAME: Are you sure?

COMIC: Yes. I'm sure.

DAME: Right. Then I'll take it all at once.

   [*She snatches the money from him and exits.*]

COMIC: Hey, that's not right. [*Runs after her.*]

This next little money gag is a real gem. It's actually not so much a gag, more comedy patter but I like it because there is a feeling that with a lot of luck and a following wind you could just get away with it in real life. The first time I heard this gag was in a production of *Cinderella* that I appeared in at Cambridge. I was very ill for most of this pantomime season and don't remember much about it but one of the few things I do remember is listening to this exchange between the Baron and the Brokers' men and thinking how funny it was. I hope you agree with me. I've called the item . . .

THE MONEY LENDING GAG

[*The* BARON *and the* BROKERS' MEN *enter from opposite sides.*]

BARON: Ah good morning gentlemen. To what do I owe the honour of this visit?

BROKERS' 1: We have come here to collect your rent.

BROKERS' 2: You owe the King seven hundred pounds.

BARON: Yes, well I'm quite willing to pay.

BROKERS' 1: Good.

BARON: But I haven't any money of my own.

BROKERS' 2: Well whose money have you got?

BROKERS' 1: We don't care whose money it is so long as you pay.

BARON: Very well then. Have you any money with you?

BROKERS' 2: I've got a hundred pounds.

BROKERS' 1: And I've got ten pounds.

BARON: Well lend me that money for a while.

BROKERS' 2: When do we get it back?

BARON: On my honour. If you are not satisfied with the transaction I'll return it immediately if not sooner.

BROKERS' 1: That sounds good enough for me.

BROKERS' 2: And me. [*They hand over the cash.*]

BARON: Now will you kindly accept one hundred and ten pounds on account of my debt to the King.

BROKERS' 1: You can't pay with that, it's our money.

BARON: You said it didn't matter whose money I paid with.

BROKERS' 2: We don't. So long as it's not ours.

BARON: In that case as you're not satisfied with the transaction I will return your cash as promised.

BROKERS' 1: Quite right too.

BARON: I'll just count it out to make sure it's all there. Who will accept it?

BROKERS' 2: I will. [*He holds his hand out.*]

BARON: Very well. Now then, one, two, three, how many years have you been in this job?

BROKERS' 2: Seven.

BARON: Eight, nine, ten, have you any family?

BROKERS' 2: No but my parents had twenty children.

BARON: How many?

BROKERS' 2: Twenty.

BARON: Twenty-one, twenty-two, twenty-three. How old are you?

BROKERS' 2: Thirty-one.

BARON: Thirty-two, thirty-three, thirty-four.

BROKERS' 2: My father's ninety.

BARON: Ninety-one, ninety-two, ninety-three.

BROKERS' 1: That's nothing, my grandmother lived until she was a hundred and five.

BARON: One hundred and six, one hundred and seven, eight, nine, ten. There you are, That's all your money back and there's no harm done.

BROKERS' 2: Thank you very much. You're a gent.

BROKERS: It's nice doing business with you. Goodbye.

BARON: Goodbye gentlemen. [*He puts the rest of the money in his pocket and they all exit in opposite directions.*]

The last money gag is very simple, as are most good ideas. It relies on the ingenuity of the people playing it and the chaos they cause when they search the audience. I have seen comedians have a whole audience in uproar with this simple but effective ploy. This is how it works.

THE FIFTY PENCE GAG

[*The* FEED *enters and announces that he will sing a song.*]

FEED: Ladies and gentlemen. I have had a request to sing a lovely old song entitled . . . [*He starts to sing the song and throughout all that follows he must keep a deadpan expression on his face and ignore completely everything that goes on around him. On no account must he stop singing.*]

[*Enter* DAME *and* COMIC.]

DAME: Well what is it that you want me to help you with?

COMIC: I've lost a fifty pence piece and I'm sure it's here somewhere. I want you to help me look for it.

DAME [*searching around the stage*]: Well I can't see anything here.

COMIC [*indicating* FEED]: I wonder if he had anything to do with it.

DAME: He might have done. Perhaps we ought to search him.

COMIC: A good idea. Let's have a look.

[*They search the* FEED *who carries on singing and totally ignores them. They take off his hat and look under it. Then remove his jacket and search that. They lift his arms to look underneath and search his trouser pockets etc.*]

DAME: Well your fifty pence isn't there, is it?

COMIC: I've just had a thought, I might have dropped it in the orchestra pit. Let's have a look.

[*They go into the orchestra pit to search the musical director. They go through his pockets pulling out all manner of strange objects. A bra perhaps, or a lavatory brush, or an old corset.*]

DAME: It's not here is it. Where else can we look?

COMIC: I suppose I could have dropped it in the audience. Let's go and have a look there.

[*The house lights come on as the pair of them go down into the audience and cause as much mayhem as possible. They make a whole row of the audience stand up whilst they search the row.*

They look under seats, in people's hats etc. If the circle is low enough they get a ladder and climb up and search there. They do anything in fact to cause total chaos.]

DAME: Well it's not here anywhere. Perhaps we'd better look out the back.

COMIC: OK, we'll have a look backstage.

[*They walk back on to the stage and as they exit the song comes to an end. The FEED moves his foot to reveal the fifty pence piece. He bends down and picks it up, winks at the audience, puts the coin in his pocket and exits.*]

I once spent a very happy three months appearing as Sarah the Cook in a production of *Dick Whittington* with Frank Carson, the Irish comedian and an old-time comic called Cardew Robinson. The producers of the piece decided that we would do this next gag, entitled 'The Magic Hat', which revolves around the idea that when you put this magic hat on your head you cannot hear a word that is said to you, so when working the gag you must silently mime the words when you put the hat on your partner's head and only speak when the hat is off his head. Cardew, although a very talented comedian and actor, found it almost impossible to work with props and having to lift the hat on and off someone's head whilst either speaking or miming only added to his confusion. He would put the hat on and start to speak then, realizing he was wrong would start to mime, thinking he was wrong again, he'd take the hat off but continue miming. The audience, knowing what should be happening, would quickly realize that he was making a complete hash of the gag and would howl with laughter at his vain attempts to work it correctly. The result was that although the gag was never worked as it should have been it still got great laughs. Over the years this has become a firm favourite of mine and when it's worked well (or not) it gets a very good response.

'The Magic Hat' involves three people: the first two set it up and the third walks right into it.

THE MAGIC HAT

[*Enter* FEEDS 1 *and* 2.]

FEED 1: Hello. You're looking very pale and red eyed, have you been on the tiles all night?

FEED 2: No I haven't. I'm just not sleeping well. The street outside my house is so noisy I can't get to sleep at night.

FEED 1: I've got something that'll help you to sleep all night without a break.

FEED 2: I'd give anything to have a full night's sleep. What is it?

FEED 1: A magic hat.

FEED 2: A magic hat. How can a magic hat stop all the noise outside my window?

FEED 1: If you listen I'll explain. This hat was given to me by an old fakir, he said that whenever you wear it you won't be able to hear a thing anybody says to you. So if you were to wear it in bed you wouldn't hear any noise and you'd get a good night's sleep, wouldn't you?

FEED 2: That sounds amazing. Do you think it'll work?

FEED 1: Of course it'll work, I can guarantee it.

FEED 2: Can I try it. I've just got to get a good night's sleep somehow.

FEED 1: Certainly you can try it. Now put it on and let's see if you can hear anything I say to you.

FEED 2: I'm all ears.

FEED 1: I had noticed that.

FEED 2: Well come on, where is this hat?

FEED 1: Here it is. [*Takes a shabby old hat out of a paper bag.*]

FEED 2: That old thing is magic?

FEED 1: It's ever so magic, I'll show you. Now there was this lady ... [*Put hat on. Mime words for a few seconds then take hat off*] ... and there she was with this bag ... [*Hat on. Mime for a few seconds. Hat off*] ... a yellow one and a red one ... [*Hat on. Mime. Hat off*] ... four pounds twenty five ... [*Hat on. Mime. Hat off*] ... and the policeman fainted. Now did you hear anything I said when you had the hat on?

FEED 2: Not a word. It's wonderful. If I were to wear that in bed I'd hear none of the noise in the street. Can I buy it?

FEED 1: Yes, if you want.

FEED 2: How much do you want for it?

FEED 1: Twenty pounds.

FEED 2: Well it's my last twenty pounds but I'm sure it'll be well worth it. Here you are.

[*He gives* FEED *the money and puts the hat on.*]

FEED 1: Thank you very much. I'm sure you'll be very satisfied. You'll get a good night's sleep and if ... [*He realizes he has spoken whilst* FEED 2 *is wearing the hat*]. Oh heck ...

FEED 2: I heard every word you said. This isn't a magic hat at all. I've been conned. I want my money back. This is a fake.

FEED 1: Well I did say I got it from a fakir.

FEED 2: I want my money back. That was my last twenty pounds. Give it back to me.

FEED 1: I can't give you your money back, but I'll help you to sell the hat and make a profit on it.

FEED 2: Who'd be daft enough to fall for a trick like this?

FEED 1: Well you did.

FEED 2: You're right, I did, so we've got to find someone as daft as me.

FEED 1: That's right.

FEED 2: Do you think we'll find anyone as daft as that?

FEED 1: It'll be difficult but we'll try.

[*Enter* COMIC.]

FEED 1 [*To* COMIC]: Hello, how are you?

COMIC: I'm fine thanks, full of the joys of spring.

FEED 2: Aren't you tired?

COMIC: No I'm not tired at all. I've had a good night's sleep.

FEED 1: You look tired.

COMIC: Do you think so?

FEED 2: Yes you do. Are you sure you're sleeping well?

COMIC: Well I did last night.

FEED 1: Ah, but do you sleep well every night?

COMIC: No, not every night, sometimes I can't get to sleep.

FEED 2: That'll be the noise.

COMIC: What noise?

FEED 2: The noise in the street that keeps you awake at night.

FEED 1: We have something here that'll help you to sleep.

COMIC: What is it?

FEED 1: It's a magic hat.

FEED 2: When you put it on your head you can't hear any noise at all and you'll get a good night's sleep.

FEED 1: And we'll sell it to you for forty pounds.

COMIC: Well, I'd need to see it working first.

FEED 2: That's no problem, we will give you a demonstration.

[*They stand one either side of the* COMIC *and go into a long garbled story as before, miming when the hat is on his head and speaking when it is off. They both take turns at putting the hat on and off and the whole thing gets very frantic. The story must not make any sense.*]

FEED 1: What did you think of that?

COMIC: I thought it was marvellous but before I hand over my forty pounds could I have just one more demonstration?

FEED 2: Of course you can and this time we'll do something very unusual.

COMIC: I hope we don't get arrested.

FEED 2: No. This time we're going to sing.

COMIC: We will get arrested.

FEED 1: We're going to sing a song entitled, 'If we had to do it all over again, we'd do it all over you.'

COMIC: My all time favourite.

> [*They sing and mime a chorus of a song. Any song will do. They alternately sing and mime the lines of the song but this time the* COMIC *is putting the hat on and off himself thereby catching the two of them out as they sing or mime.*]

FEED 1: What do you think?

COMIC: It's great. I'll take it. [*He starts to exit wearing the hat.*]

FEED 2: Hey, where's our forty pounds?

FEED 1: Come back, we want our money.

COMIC: I'm sorry, I can't hear a thing with this hat on. [*Exit.*]

To get the most out of a pantomime gag and to show it to its best advantage the performer must act at all times as if he believes in the situation created by the gag. Just as some children believe in Father Christmas and the Tooth Fairy so there will be some children in the audience who believe in pantomime. They will believe that the girl in tights playing Aladdin or Dick Whittington is really a boy and the Dame is really a silly old woman. They will also believe in the plot, that Cinderella really does go to the ball and King Rat does indeed sink Dick Whittington's ship. It is therefore essential that we do nothing to dispel this belief. Childhood innocence is a beautiful thing and should be preserved for as long as possible. Having said that, the mind boggles at the thought of a young child believing that this next situation could really happen, but some of them will. 'The Pheasant Gag' is a very old four-handed gag that I first remember seeing in a pantomime at the Empire Theatre, Chatham; from about the age of five I was taken there every year to see the Christmas production.

THE PHEASANT GAG

[*Enter* FEED 1.]

FEED 1 [*To audience*]: I've just received a present from my auntie; she's sent a letter with it as well. It says 'I hope you have a happy Christmas and enjoy this present of a pheasant. [*He is holding a bag with some tail feathers of a pheasant sticking out. He opens the bag and looks in.*] Phew, it stinks, it must have gone off in the post. I'll have to get rid of this. I wonder who I can give it to.

[*Enter* FEED 2.]

FEED 2: Hello. What have you got there?

FEED 1: Oh this is a beautiful pheasant and I'd like to give it to you as a present. You can have it for your dinner. [*He hands it over.*]

FEED 2: Why, thank you very much, that's very kind of you.

FEED 1: Don't mention it, you're welcome.

[*He exits.*]

FEED 2: I do like pheasant. [*He opens the bag and looks in.*] Cor, what a rotten stink, it's gone orft. I must get rid of this.

[*Enter* DAME.]

DAME: Hello. Have you been doing your shopping?

FEED 2: No, er, yes. Actually I brought this for you. It's a present of a pheasant, I thought you might like it for your supper.

[*He hands it over and exits quickly.*]

DAME: A present of a pheasant, how very very pleasant. I'll put it in a casserole.

[*She opens the bag and sticks her nose in.*]

Lummy, what a pong. It's an unpleasant pheasant. I must get rid of this as quick as I can.

[*Enter the* COMIC.]

COMIC: Hello, have you been to the sales?

DAME: Yes I have and I've bought you a little gift.

COMIC: Is it something that's advertised on television?

DAME: No, but it's something that's advertised on smelly-vision.

COMIC: What is it?

DAME: It's a present of a pheasant.

[*She hands it over to him.*] And I hope you'll both be very happy together. [*She exits.*]

COMIC: A present of a pheasant. I've never eaten pheasant before, I wonder how you cook it. I'll have it with chips. [*He opens the bag and gets a whiff.*] Bloomin' heck, this one's had his chips. Cor dear, it smells as if it hasn't changed its socks for a year. I'd better get rid of it somewhere.

[*He exits one side as* FEED 1 *enters from the opposite side.*]

FEED 1 [*to audience*]: I've just been reading this letter from my auntie. She says she's put a twenty pound note under the pheasant. I must try to get it back.

[*Enter* FEED 2.] Have you got that pheasant I gave you?

FEED 2: No, it was rotten, I gave it away.

FEED 1: Well my auntie said she had put a twenty pound note under it. I must get it back.

FEED 2: Well, I gave it to the Dame. [*Enter* DAME.] Ah, here she is now. Have you got that pheasant I gave you?

DAME: No I haven't. It smelt 'orrible. Why do you ask?

FEED 2: It's got a twenty pound note under it. We must try to get it back.

DAME: Oh heck, I gave it to . . . (COMIC). [*Enter* COMIC *holding bag with pheasant in it.*] Thank goodness, here he is.

[*She snatches the bag from him.*]

I've got the pheasant.

FEED 2 [*snatches the bag from the* DAME]: I've got the pheasant.

FEED 1 [*snatches the bag from* FEED 2]: I've got the pheasant.
COMIC [*holding up a note*]: Yes, but I've got the twenty pound note.
　　　[*Black-out.*]

You may already have realized that gags do not have to be long to be funny. Brevity is said to be the 'soul of wit', a view with which most comedians would concur. Here follows a gag which is very brief indeed – about ten seconds – but is worth including in a show as it gets a very big laugh. It is best performed by the Dame or Ugly Sisters but any female comedy character could work it.

THE FISHING GAG

[*The* DAME *enters with a fishing rod. Without saying a word she sits on the edge of the stage and starts to fish in the orchestra pit. The* FEED *enters.*]

FEED: What on earth are you up to?

DAME: I'm fishing for a man.

FEED: You won't catch a man like that.

DAME: Oh yes I will.

[*She pulls her fishing rod out of the pit and on the hook is a suit of man's clothes. A stooge, dressed only in his undies, jumps out of the pit and runs up the centre aisle and out of the auditorium complaining loudly.*]

[*Black-out.*]

Some years ago I went to Newcastle to appear in pantomime at the beautiful old Theatre Royal. I had rented a flat for the season and the landlady would appear every week to collect the rent in person. Every time she called I would be almost mesmerized by the sight of this creature. She was not very tall, about 5' 4" I would guess, in her late fifties or early sixties with badly dyed blonde hair which always had at least an inch of dark roots showing. She always wore a rather grubby but very expensive full-length mink coat and had several valuable diamond rings on her unwashed fingers which served to focus attention on her badly broken and unkempt fingernails. On her feet she invariably wore a filthy pair of purple fake fur slippers with no stockings or tights.

In all her visits, during the three months I was in the show, she was never without a cigarette protruding from between her lips and which she never appeared to remove. Proof of this fact was a dark brown nicotine stain prominent above her top lip. When the cigarette had burnt right down and was in danger of melting her thick, blood-red lipstick, she would remove the stub and immediately replace it with a new gasper. Then she'd strike a match to light it with, which would stay burning between her fingers while she talked to me about the problems of being a poor widow. She always had to strike at least three matches before she could stop talking long enough to get one of them up to the cigarette to ignite it. The others would burn down until a sharp pain in her thumb and forefinger would trigger an automatic flick of the wrist which would extinguish the flame.

The reason for this preamble is that whenever I see the following sketch performed it never fails to bring memories of this Geordie landlady flooding back. Needless to say this gag is all about lighting a cigarette.

THE MATCH GAG

[*Enter* DAME *and* FEED]

FEED: I went to an amazing football match the other day. Would you like to hear about it?

DAME: Yes I would. I like football, I've been known to have a dribble myself.

FEED: Here, have a cigarette. [*Gives* DAME *a cigarette.*]

DAME: Thank you very much. [*She lights a match but before she can put the match to her cigarette the* FEED *puts his hand on her arm, thus preventing her from putting the match to her cigarette. He then starts telling the story of the football match. Every time the* DAME *goes to put the match to her cigarette the* FEED *puts his hand on her arm preventing her from doing so. This happens two or three times until the match burns down and burns her fingers. She drops the match.*

DAME: Ow. What was that?

FEED: Oh. That was the end of the match.

[*He exits laughing.*]

DAME: That was terrible. I've burnt my fingers. Oh look, here comes . . . [COMIC'*s name*]. I'll try it out on him.

[*Enter* COMIC.]

COMIC: Hello. What are you up to?

DAME: I was just telling the boys and girls about a football match I saw yesterday. Would you like to hear about it?

COMIC: Yes I would. I love football. Did you hear that the police caught four lads trying to get over the wall at . . .[*local team's name*] . . . ground last Saturday.

DAME: Did they really?

COMIC: Yes they did, but they made them get back down and finish watching the match.

DAME: Never mind them. Here have a cigarette while I tell you about this game. [*She gives him a cigarette.*]

COMIC: Thanks very much. [*He strikes a match. This is a trick match which consists of a real match fixed on to a long taper which is hidden up the sleeve of his costume. The* DAME *starts the long story about the football match. As before, everytime the* COMIC *tries to put the match to his cigarette she puts her hand on his arm to prevent him. The story goes on and on with the* DAME *getting more and more exhausted. The match, of course, keeps on burning as the taper is very long and the* COMIC *is feeding it out as it burns. Eventually the* DAME *is worn out and can go on no longer. As she collapses to the floor she says*]:

DAME: And that's the end of the match.

COMIC: That's the end of the match. Oh no it's not, I've got miles of it here. [*He pulls the remainder of the taper out of his sleeve.*]

[*Black-out.*]

Humour has often been based on misfortune. How often have we laughed at the man who trips over something, gets a custard pie in the face or loses his trousers. Other comedians tell jokes of how their wife or boss causes them to have a terrible life or how they lost the winning lottery ticket and we fall about with laughter. We certainly seem to have a sadistic taste in comedy which seems to start from when we are very young indeed, watching cartoon characters bash each other over the head with hammers or push each other over cliffs. This next gag is no exception, for it relies for its laughs on everybody getting wet. As with most of the other gags in this book it's a very old piece and has been around in one form or another for well over a hundred years. It was another gag that was part of that first pantomime I ever appeared in over thirty years ago. Since then I have seen several versions of it and include two of them here. The gag is called:

THE TIDDLEY TREE

[FEED 1 *and* COMIC *enter.*]

COMIC: This is a funny old place isn't it?

FEED 1: Yes, but look what's here.

COMIC: What's where?

FEED 1: Here. It's the Tiddley Tree.

COMIC: The whatley tree?

FEED 1: The Tiddley Tree. It's a magic tree. If ever you are thirsty just ask the tree and it'll give you a drink.

COMIC: I don't believe that.

FEED 1: Well why don't you try it? All you have to do is stand in front of the tree and say, 'Tiddley Tree, Tiddley Tree, have you a nice little drink for me?' And you'll get one.

COMIC: Very well, I'll try it. Now I stand here and I say 'Tiddley Tree, Tiddley Tree, have you a nice little drink for me?' [*Water squirts out from the tree all over the* COMIC. FEED 1 *exits laughing.*] That's not a drink, that's a bath. I've got to go and get dried off now.

[*Enter* FEED 2.]

FEED 2: Hello. What's the matter with you?

COMIC: Oh nothing. It's just rather hot and I'm perspiring.

FEED 2: You're right, it is rather hot. I'm so thirsty.

COMIC: I can help you out there. This tree is a magic tree and if you ask it nicely it'll give you a drink.

FEED 2: Will it really? What do I have to do?

COMIC: Just stand here and say, 'Tiddley Tree, Tiddley Tree, have you a nice little drink for me?' And you'll get one.

FEED 2: That's great. I'll have a go at that. Tiddley Tree, Tiddley Tree, have you a nice little drink for me?

[*Water squirts over* FEED 2. COMIC *exits laughing.*] That wasn't very nice. I'm going to get my own back on someone.

[*Enter* DAME.]

DAME: At last. I thought I'd never get here. I wish I'd packed a bottle of gin.

FEED 2: If it's a drink you're after I think I can help you there.

DAME: Have you got a bottle hidden about your person?

FEED 2: No, but I've got a magic tree.

DAME: A magic tree. Where have you hidden that?

FEED 2: I haven't. It's there.

DAME: What's magic about that?

FEED 2: If you stand in front of it and say 'Tiddley Tree, Tiddley Tree, have you a nice little drink for me?', you'll get one.

DAME: If I say it twice will I get a double?

FEED 2: Oh don't worry. You'll get plenty.

DAME: I'll have a try. Tiddley Tree, Tiddley Tree, have you a bloomin' great drink for me? [*She gets the water.* FEED 2 *exits.*] What a mess. Just wait till I get my hands on him.

[*Enter* COMIC.]

COMIC: What's happened to you?

DAME: Nothing's happened to me.

COMIC: But you're all wet.

DAME: I'm not wet. I was thinking about my dinner and my mouth's watering.

COMIC: Looks like it watered all over you.

[*He goes to exit.*]

DAME: Before you go, would you like a drink with me?

COMIC: No thanks, I'm not thirsty.

DAME: Oh but you must be. Come along, have a little drinky winky with me.

COMIC [*gives knowing look to audience*]: All right then, I'll have a drink.

DAME: Good. All you have to do is stand in front of this magic tree and say, 'Tiddley Tree, Tiddley Tree, have you a nice little drink for me?' And you'll get it.

COMIC: I'll get it, will I?

DAME: Oh yes, you'll get it all right. Now come along, let's hear it.

COMIC: Tiddley Tree, Tiddley Tree [*he walks forward*] have you a nice little drink for me? [*The water squirts behind him.*]

DAME: No, no, no. You mustn't move. Say it all standing still.

COMIC: All right, I'll stand still. [*He stands in line with the tree but a long way from it.*] Tiddley Tree, Tiddley Tree, have you a nice little drink for me? [*The water squirts but doesn't reach him.*]

DAME: No, no, no. You stand here. [*She pushes him in position.*] You do not move. You just say the lines.

COMIC: OK, I'll stand here and say the lines.

DAME: Yes, and I'll stand over here, out of the way. Beside this other tree. [*She stands the other side of the stage, beside another tree.*]

COMIC: Tiddley Tree, Tiddley Tree, errrr. I've forgotten it.

DAME: You really are a plonker. All you say is 'Tiddley Tree, Tiddley Tree, have you a nice little drink for me?' [*Her tree now squirts her with water. She chases the* COMIC *off.*]

This is a second version of the same gag. The difference this time is that it is only the Comic who gets squirted with water. All the other participants get the drink they have asked for.

THE TIDDLEY TREE

SECOND VERSION

[*Enter* DAME *and* COMIC.]

COMIC: I still don't believe you. A magic tree indeed.

DAME: It's true, look, here it is. [*Points to tree.*]

COMIC: It looks like any old tree to me. What's it supposed to do?

DAME: All you've got to do is to say 'Tiddley Tree, Tiddley Tree, have you a nice little drink for me?' And it gives you a drink.

COMIC: I don't know about that. I've been caught out before. You try it first.

DAME: Oh very well, here goes. 'Tiddley Tree, Tiddley Tree, have you a nice little drink for me?' [*A branch of the tree reaches out and hands her a bottle of drink.*] There you are, I told you.

COMIC: That's brilliant. Get out of the way. I want to have a go. [*He pushes her out of the way.*] Tiddley Tree, Tiddley Tree, have you a nice little drink for me? [*The tree squirts him with water.* DAME *laughs and exits.*] That's not fair, I must have said it wrong, I'll try it again. [*Enter* FEED 1.]

FEED 1: What devious deeds are you up to?

COMIC: I'm not up to anything. I'm just talking to this magic tree.

FEED 1: Talking to trees. You need a lie down.

COMIC: No it's true, this tree is magic. If you go up to it and say 'Tiddley Tree, Tiddley Tree, have you a nice little drink for me?' you'll get one.

FEED 1: Really, Well I must have a go at that. [*He goes up to tree and speaks.*] Tiddley Tree, Tiddley Tree, have you a nice little drink for me? [*The branch hands him a bottle of drink.*] Thank you very much. [*He exits.*]

COMIC: Right, it's working properly now, I'll have another go. Tiddley tree, tiddley tree, have you a nice little drink for me. [*He gets squirted with water again.*] Ow, it's still going wrong. What can I do?

[*Enter* FEED 2.] Hey, do you want to see a magic tree?

FEED 2: A magic tree. What does it do?

COMIC: I'll show you. Come here and stand next to me. [FEED 2 *stands next to* COMIC.] Now listen to this. Tiddley Tree, Tiddley Tree, have you a nice little drink for me? [*He steps out of the way and pushes the* FEED *into his place. The* FEED *gets a bottle of drink.*]

FEED 2: Why thank you very much, that's lovely.

COMIC: I've got it right at last. Get out of the way. [*He pushes the* FEED *out of the way.*] Tiddley Tree, Tiddley Tree, have you a nice little drink for me? [*As usual he gets soaked.*] I don't believe it. [FEED *laughs and exits. Enter* DAME.]

DAME: Goodness me, what on earth has happened to you? You look as if you've been caught in a storm.

COMIC: It's this rotten, so called, magic tree of yours. It keeps soaking me with water.

DAME: You must be saying the words wrong. Listen to me. Tiddley Tree, Tiddley Tree, have you a piece of fruit for me? [*The tree hands her an orange.*]

COMIC: You said it different that time.

DAME: Of course, it gives you what you ask for. I asked for fruit and it gave me an orange.

COMIC: Perhaps that's what's wrong I should try asking for something else. [*He goes up to the tree.*] Tiddley Tree, Tiddley Tree, have you a nice cup of tea for me? [*The tree holds out a cup of tea but as he goes to take it it throws the tea in his face.*]

DAME: Try asking it for some fruit like I did.

COMIC: I'll ask it for fruit then, but if it soaks me with water this time I'll chop it down. [*He goes over to tree.*] Now listen to me, Tiddley Tree, I want some fruit, like her, so give it to me. [*A great load of oranges fall from the top of the tree hitting him on the head. As he falls over there is a black-out.*]

Another wet gag that follows in the wake of 'The Tiddley Tree' is the 'Busy Bee Gag'. This involves rushing on and off stage with mouthfuls of water so two large glasses of water must be set just off stage, one either side. The format is the same as in a lot of these gags: the Comic gets caught first, then after he catches out two or three others the Dame tries to catch him out, not realizing that he already knows the gag. I did this gag one year with David Jason and two other very fine actors, Sylvester McCoy and David Rappaport; unfortunately none of us were a very good aim with the water and subsequently the orchestra tended to get very wet, until one night just as we started the routine as usual we noticed that the whole orchestra had put up umbrellas.

THE BUSY BEE

[*Enter* FEED 1 *and* COMIC.]

COMIC: I'm glad I've bumped into you. Are you going anywhere near a shop?

FEED 1: Why, what do you want?

COMIC: I want something for my tea.

FEED 1: How about some honey?

COMIC: I love honey.

FEED 1: I know how you can get some honey for nothing.

COMIC: Free honey, how?

FEED 1: All you've got to do is say 'Busy bee, busy bee, what have you got in the hive for me?' and you'll get it.

COMIC: Is that all I have to do?

FEED 1: Yes, that's all there is to it. We'll have a practice. I'll be the bee. I'll go off and come buzzing back on and you say it.

COMIC: OK. Off you go then. [FEED *exits and gets a mouthful of water.* COMIC *speaks to audience.*] Isn't this exciting, free honey. [FEED *enters buzzing like a bee.*] Busy bee, busy bee, what have you got in the hive for me? [FEED *spits water over him and exits laughing.*] What a rotten trick! [*Enter* FEED 2.]

FEED 2: What's happened to you? You look like you've fallen in the sink.

COMIC: I have, I was tap dancing and I fell in.

FEED 2: Really?

COMIC: No of course not. I've just been eating some free honey.

FEED 2: Free honey, I'd like some of that.

COMIC: Well all you have to say is 'Busy bee, busy bee, what have you got in the hive for me?' And you'll get it.

FEED 2: How lovely, I'll have a go at that.

COMIC: We'll have a rehearsal. I'll be the bee. I'll buzz off and buzz on again. [*He exits to get a mouthful of water.*]

FEED 2: Now, I mustn't forget what I've got to say. [*Enter* COMIC.] Right, here goes: Busy bee, busy bee, what have you got in the hive for me? [COMIC *spits water over him and exits laughing.*] That wasn't very nice. I'm going to have a go at that. [*Enter* DAME.] Hello, do you like free food?

DAME: Free food? Of course I do. What have you got?

FEED 2: I can tell you how to get some free honey.

DAME: Well carry on then. Tell me.

FEED 2: All you have to do is to go to the magic hive and say, 'Busy bee, busy bee, what have you got in the hive for me?' and you'll get it.

DAME: I want it. I want it. Where's this magic hive?

FEED 2: We'll have to practise first. I'll be the bee. I'll be off and be back soon. [*He exits to get a mouthful of water.*]

DAME: Well don't be long. I want the honey, honey. [FEED 2 *re-enters.*] Busy bee, busy bee, give me something for my tea. [*He spits the water over her and exits.*] Ugh. you're disgusting. If I wasn't such a lady I'd give you a slap in the gob. [*Enter* COMIC.] Ah, just the man I want to see.

COMIC: Well you've seen me. Now what do you want?

DAME: Would you like some free honey, for nothing? It's going cheap.

COMIC [*with a knowing look to the audience*]: I think I've heard of this free offer before.

DAME: Well, come on, do you want some or not?

COMIC: Go on then. Tell me, what do I have to do?

DAME: You go to a little house where the bees live and you say 'Busy bee, busy bee, what have you got in the hive for me?' and you'll get it.

COMIC: I bet I won't.

DAME: Oh yes you will.

COMIC [*urging audience to shout*]: Oh no I won't.

DAME: Oh yes you will.

COMIC: Oh no I won't.

DAME: I'll prove it to you. Let's have a rehearsal. I'll be the busy bee.

COMIC: And I'll be the silly b. [*The* DAME *exits for a mouthful of water. As soon as she is out of sight the* COMIC *exits off the other side and gets a mouthful of water. They both enter at the same time and stand there facing each other unable to speak. The* DAME *indicates to the* COMIC *that he should speak but he just stands there. After a few tries at getting him to speak the* DAME *has to swallow her water.*]

DAME: You're supposed to say, 'Busy bee, busy bee, what have you got in the hive for me?' [COMIC *swallows his water.*]

COMIC: I'm so sorry, I forgot.

DAME: Well don't forget this time. We'll have another go. [*She exits for water, as does the* COMIC. *This time as they enter from opposite sides the* COMIC *accidentally trips and falls on his face spitting out his water. This makes the* DAME *laugh and she has to spit her water out. They both run off for more. This time they enter and stand next to one another. The* DAME *tries to get the* COMIC *to say the words by humming them. She tries this several times whilst the* COMIC, *with his mouthful of water, looks at her pityingly. In the end, in desperation, she has to swallow her water.*] You are supposed to say, 'Busy bee, busy bee, what have you got in the hive for me?' [*The* COMIC *spits his water over her and runs off laughing.*]

[*Black-out.*]

Pantomime gags are at their best when they are visual. Funny props, costumes and wigs are the mainstay of most pantomimes. This next routine has both visual and verbal gags which ensure it gets good reaction from both the adults and the children. When making props for visual gags, always make them larger and more colourful than in reality. This way you'll find that just bringing on the prop will get a giggle even before you get to the gag itself. In this routine two sandwiches are used; they should be made of foam rubber and be at least three times the size of a normal sandwich. Similarly, the bottle of wine that is used should be a very large bottle; the inflatable bottles that can be brought in joke shops are ideal. With the right props this next routine gets very big laughs. It involves three characters: the Dame, the Comic and one other.

THE PICNIC

[*Enter* DAME, COMIC *and* FEED.]

COMIC: I'm starving, I feel as if I haven't eaten for days.

FEED: Yes, I could do with a bite.

DAME: You two are always hungry. Well, you're in luck. I've brought a little picnic with me.

COMIC: Oh good. Where is it?

DAME [*pulling on very large theatrical skip*]: Here's the hamper.

FEED: It looks like she's packed up half of Tesco's.

DAME: It's only a few sandwiches.

COMIC: A few sandwiches, in a dirty great basket like that.

DAME: Yes, well, I used thick sliced bread. [*To* COMIC.] Anyway, I thought you were on a diet.

COMIC: I am. All I eat is salad oil, vegetable oil and sunflower oil.

FEED: Have you lost any weight?

COMIC: No, but I don't squeak anymore.

[*They sit down round the basket at one side of the stage beside the proscenium arch.*]

FEED: Well, I want a sandwich. What sort have you packed?

DAME: I was going to do turkey.

COMIC: Oh good, I like turkey.

DAME: But I forgot. I've got the turkey and I've already plucked it and stuffed it. All I've got to do now is kill it and cook it.

COMIC: She's a terrible cook you know. You've heard of Cordon Bleu cooking? Well, her cooking's cordoned off.

FEED: She can't be that bad.

COMIC: She baked a cake once and Rentokil bought the recipe off her.

DAME: Don't be cheeky.

COMIC: When she serves gravy she asks if you like one lump or two.

DAME: I'll thump you in a minute. [*To* FEED.] I've put a nice bottle of wine in for us. [*She pulls out a giant bottle.*]

FEED: What type is it?

DAME: It's a cross between Muscatel and Hock.

COMIC: What's it called?

DAME: Muck.

COMIC: Can I have a sandwich? [*She hands him a very large sandwich which is attached to a fishing line which goes offstage.*] What's in it?

DAME: Fish paste. [*As he goes to bite into the sandwich the line is pulled from offstage and the sandwich flies off.*]

COMIC: Blimey. It must be flying fish paste.

FEED: May I try one?

DAME: Here you are. [*Hands him a sandwich with another trick line on.*] That one's pork.

[*As he goes to take a bite the sandwich flies offstage.*]

FEED: I bet that was leg of pork.

DAME: You're right. How did you know?

FEED: Well it's just legged it.

DAME: Would you like some asparagus tips?

COMIC: No thanks, I've given up smoking.

DAME: Oh you are higorant. You'd live on baked beans if I let you.

COMIC: I know a poem about baked beans, would you like to hear it?

DAME: Oh, if we must.

COMIC: We have baked beans for breakfast,
           We have baked beans for tea.
           We eat loads and loads of baked beans,
           My brother Billy and me.
           We eat loads and loads of baked beans,
           Enough to fill a cart.
           And when you've had as many baked beans

As me,

There's no room for apple tart.

DAME: Behave yourself. [*To* FEED.] Here, have a meat pie. [*She hands him a large pie.*]

FEED: There's a worm in this pie.

DAME: Where?

FEED: There, look. [*As the* DAME *looks a giant worm appears to run out of the pie and all round the proscenium arch. This is achieved by fixing screw eyes all around the arch and threading fishing line all through them with the end offstage. Tie your worm, about twelve inches long, to the other end of the line, making sure it is flexible enough to go through the screw eyes. When the offstage end of the line is pulled the worm travels through the screw eyes all round the arch to offstage. Make sure the worm starts at floor level on the side of the stage where the action is set. Place the pie on the floor in front of the worm just before the start of the gag.*]

DAME: Boy, that was a big worm.

FEED: So it should be, it's eaten all the meat.

DAME: Never mind, I've made a lovely sherry trifle. [*She hands it to the* COMIC.] You can smell the sherry in it.

COMIC: So you can. [*As he goes to sniff the trifle a* GORILLA *enters and pushes his face into it.*] Ow, don't do that.

DAME/FEED: We didn't do it.

COMIC [*to audience*]: Well who did?

[*Kids shout 'A gorilla did'.*]

DAME: Don't be daft, you don't get gorillas here. [*Hands* FEED *a real banana.*] Have a banana.

FEED: Thank you, I like bananas. [*He peels it and the* GORILLA *enters and breaks the top off it. He speaks to* COMIC.] You've eaten half my banana.

COMIC: I didn't touch your nana. Did I kids? [*Kids all shout 'No it was the gorilla'.*]

FEED: Well I don't care what they say. I'm not sitting next to you anymore. I don't trust you. [*He stands behind them and goes to eat the rest of his banana. The* GORILLA *enters and roars.*]

DAME: There's no need for manners like that. [*The* FEED *sees the* GORILLA, *which then chases him off. The other two don't notice this action. The* DAME *speaks to the* COMIC.] Here, would you like a banana?

COMIC: Oh lovely, thank you very much. [*The* COMIC *stands up and peels his banana. The* GORILLA *enters again and grabs his hand as he goes to take a bite. The* GORILLA *then puts his other arm round the* COMIC's *waist as if he's going to squeeze him, but instead they go into a waltz and both dance off. The* DAME *then looks round but can't see him.*]

DAME [*to audience*]: Where has he gone? [*Kids shout 'the Gorilla took him'.*] Oh no he didn't.

KIDS: Oh yes he did.

DAME: Oh no he didn't.

KIDS: Oh yes he did.

DAME: Well I think I'd better tidy everything up and go looking for the pair of them. [*As she is putting things into the skip the* GORILLA *enters and pushes her into it. He then spins it round the stage and pushes it off. The* DAME *has her legs hanging out of the skip and is, of course, screaming and shouting.*]

There are many routines and gags in pantomime that have become classics over the years. There are also stories about pantomime that have become classics as well. The most famous must be the one concerning Cilla Black when appearing in *Jack and the Beanstalk* at Birmingham. She would chop down the beanstalk and the giant would fall, 'What shall I do with him?' she'd ask and the audience would shout back 'Kill him'. 'How shall I kill him?' continued Cilla. One night a lone voice bellowed 'Sing to it.'

This next routine is also, to my mind, a classic pantomime gag. It is quite ridiculous, but for a fleeting moment seems to work out. This one is also mainly visual and therefore not easy to write down, which is probably why I've never seen it in print before. Everyone I asked about this gag knew of it; indeed most of them had worked it at some time or other but no one could remember exactly how it worked. Consequently I spent hours fiddling with the props before I worked out the modus operandi. This version uses three people and three hats.

3 X 3 = 10

COMIC [*to audience*]: I wish I could think of a way to earn some money. I'm down to my last fiver. I've always been poor. When I was a kid we were so poor my mum used to take the bones out of her corset to make a pot of stew.

    [*Enter* FEED.]

FEED: Ah, there you are. I've been looking for you.

COMIC: Well now that you've found me, what do you want?

FEED: Tell me, were you clever at school?

COMIC: Me clever? I was the teacher's pet. She used to keep me in a cage at the back of the room.

FEED: Well if you can answer me a simple question you could win some money.

COMIC: Just what I wanted to hear. How can I win some money? Tell me. Tell me.

FEED: Well, I bet you five pounds that you can't tell me what three times three equals.

COMIC: That's easy, I know that.

FEED: Well put your money down then.

[COMIC *puts down a fiver*.]

COMIC: Now all I've got to do is tell you the answer to three times three?

FEED: That's right, go on.

COMIC: This is easy money. Three times three is nine. Give me your money.

FEED: Just a minute. You're wrong. Three times three is ten.

COMIC: What are you talking about, it's nine.

FEED: I'll prove to you that three times three is ten. Lend me your hat. [*He takes the* COMIC's *hat and his own*.] We need another hat. [*To musical director*.] Have you got a hat we can borrow? [*M.D. passes up a hat*.]

COMIC: How can you prove that three times three is ten with three hats?

FEED: It's simple, look. [*He puts the three hats on the floor in a line and points to them in turn from left to right as he counts*.] One, two, three. [*He now points to the centre hat as he continues*.] Four, five. [*On counting five he picks up the hat on the left, followed by the other two as he counts*.] Six, seven, [*He now has all three hats in his hands which he now drops on the floor in a line as he counts*.] Eight, nine, ten. There you are, three times three is ten.

[*He picks up the money and exits*.]

COMIC: What a swindle. I've lost my last fiver now. What am I going to do?

[*Enter* DAME.]

DAME: What are you moaning about?

COMIC [*realizing he has a chance of getting his money back*]: I'm not moaning. I've just thought of a way you could win some money.

DAME: That's very kind of you. I could do with some more money. Do you realize food has gone up to nearly twelve pounds a bottle? Tell me how I can win some money.

COMIC: It's easy. I bet you a fiver you can't tell me what three times three equals.

DAME: That's easy, I can answer that.

COMIC: Well put your fiver down then. [*She puts her money down*.] Now three times three is ten.

DAME: No it isn't.

COMIC: Yes it is, three times three is ten.

DAME: How do you work that out?

COMIC: I'll show you. [*He goes through the same counting routine with the three hats as before. Then picks up her money and goes to exit.*]

DAME: Just a minute, come back here. Three times three is not ten.

DAME: Well what is it then?

DAME: It's eleven.

COMIC: It's what?

DAME: Three times three is eleven.

COMIC: If you can prove that I'll eat all the hats.

DAME: Put the fiver down then. [*He does so.*] Now watch this. [*She puts the three hats on the floor in a line and points from left to right as she counts.*] One, two, three. [*She points to the third hat again as she continues counting.*] Four, five. [*She picks up the hat on the left as she counts.*] Six. [*Then picks up the other two as she counts.*] Seven, eight. [*Now she drops the three hats on the floor, one at a time, as she counts.*] Nine, ten, eleven. [*She picks up the money and the hats and hands the hats to the* COMIC *as she exits.*] Here, do you want these boiled or fried?

[*Black-out.*]

Here's a nice little four-handed routine which, like most of the gags in this book, seems to have been around for ever. As with the last gag it is mainly visual and involves a lot of throwing and dropping of parcels, which audiences love to see.

The only time I have performed this routine was in pantomime at Plymouth many years ago. Now in Plymouth at the time was a distillery owned by a small family firm that made gin. The pantomime company was invited, one morning, to look around the said distillery to see how gin and vodka were made. The process is fairly simple and in no time at all we had looked at everything there was to see and had been ushered into a beautiful hospitality room to sample the wares. The gin and vodka flowed freely and we all imbibed for much longer than was sensible on a matinée day. Eventually we all staggered up the road from the 'Gin Factory' to the theatre to start the afternoon performance. All went well, if slightly laboured, until we came to the following gag where the parcel has to be thrown around the stage as per the script. The first person to throw it dropped it, and as he bent down to pick it up, fell on top of it, where he lay giggling while the rest of us tried to get the parcel out from under him so that we could carry on with the gag. This we managed to do but we couldn't lift the actor, so left him lying on the floor while we laughed our way through the remainder of the sketch to bemused stares from the audience. Now normally if something like this were to happen during a performance the company manager would read the riot act to the people involved, but none of us got carpeted this time because the actor on the floor just happened to be the company manager.

To perform this gag you will need a parcel consisting of a biscuit tin containing broken crockery. The lid must be held on securely with sticky tape and the whole thing wrapped in several layers of brown paper and tied with string. Once you have this prop you are ready to perform . . .

THE PARCEL GAG

[*The* DAME *enters with a parcel under her arm. As she walks across the stage* FEED 1 *enters and they meet.*]
FEED 1: Hello, where are you dashing off to?

DAME: I'm off to the post office to post this parcel.

FEED 1: Really. What's in it?

DAME: It's a twenty-one-piece dinner service.

FEED 1: A twenty-one-piece dinner service. I wouldn't send that by post.

DAME: Why ever not?

FEED 1: Well look. I'll show you what happens. The postman takes the parcel off you and he throws it in his sack. [FEED *takes parcel from* DAME *and drops it on the floor*.] Then he throws the sack over his shoulder. [*He picks up the parcel and throws it over his shoulder*.] Then when it gets to the sorting office they stamp it like this. [*Picks up parcel from floor and bashes it with his fist*.] Then they throw it in another sack to deliver it. [*Throws parcel over his shoulder*.] So I wouldn't send it by post. I mean, you don't want it to get damaged do you? [*Exit*.]

DAME: No I don't want it damaged.

   [*She picks up the parcel. Enter* FEED 2.]

FEED 2: What have you got there?

DAME: It's a ... [*Shakes parcel*] ... forty-eight-piece dinner service. I'm sending it to a friend.

FEED 2: How are you going to send it?

DAME: I thought I'd send it by airmail.

FEED 2: Oh I wouldn't send it by airmail.

DAME: Why, what's wrong with airmail?

FEED 2: I'll show you, [*Takes parcel*.] When a parcel goes by airmail the luggage man takes it and throws it into the plane. [*Throws parcel across stage*.] Then as the plane is flying it always hits bad weather and the parcels get shaken around. [*Picks up parcel and shakes it from side to side*.] Then when it gets to the other end the luggage man in the plane throws it to the man on the ground. [*He throws the parcel on the floor*.] So I wouldn't send it by airmail. I mean, you wouldn't like it to end up with one of the cups chipped would you? [*Exit*.]

DAME: He's right. I wouldn't want to get one of the cups chipped.

   [*Enter* COMIC.]

COMIC: Hello. What's that you've got there?

DAME: It's a ninety-eight-piece dinner service. It's a present for a friend and I'm going to send it to him by boat.

COMIC: You can't send a fragile parcel like that by boat.

DAME: Well I don't really know why I can't but I expect you're going to show me.

COMIC: Of course I am. [*Takes parcel.*] When a parcel goes by boat the man on the shore throws it to the man on the boat.

DAME: I thought perhaps he might.

COMIC: And the man on the boat is never any good at catching so he misses it, like this. [*He throws the parcel across the stage.*] Then the man on the boat carries it over to the hold and on the way there he trips over a rope and drops it. [*Does trip and drops the parcel.*] Then he goes over to the hold and drops it in. [*Holds parcel above head and drops it.*] But there is a man in the hold and your parcel lands on his foot and he is not very pleased.

DAME: I thought he wouldn't be. What does he do?

COMIC: He kicks it. [*He kicks parcel.*] When the boat gets to the other end the man in the hold throws it to the man outside. [*Throws parcel up in the air.*] Then he throws it to the man on the dock. [*Throws it again.*] And he throws it into his van to deliver it. [*Throws parcel once again.*] So I wouldn't send it by boat. I mean you don't want it to get cracked do you.

DAME: Oh I definitely don't want it cracked.

COMIC: What did you say it was?

DAME: It's a seven-hundred-piece dinner service.

COMIC: Oh well if it's a fragile thing like that you'd better be careful with it. It would be terrible if it turned up slightly damaged, wouldn't it?

DAME: You could be right.

COMIC: I've had an idea. Why don't you deliver it personally.

DAME: What a good idea, I think I will.

COMIC: Who's it for anyway?

DAME: It's a birthday present for you. [*Hands him the parcel.*]
   [*Black-out.*]

There seem to be many gags that revolve around one of the team trying to get money out of the others and this next one is no different. It is, however, not used very often; in fact I have only come across it once in all the years I've been interested in pantomime. I can't imagine why this should be as it's a very good routine and could get big laughs. Here it is then; it's a betting gag involving a comic and two feeds trying to win money by guessing which number is being pointed to on a numbered board.

THE NUMBER BOARD

FEED 1 [*to audience*]: I'm fed up with having no money. I'm so broke that if Woolworths were selling five pound notes for four pounds each, I couldn't afford to buy any. Mind you, that might all be about to change. I have invented this number board, and with any luck it'll make me rich.

[*He shows the audience the number board which is about one metre square and is divided into nine squares. Each square has a number from one to nine painted in it. They are in no particular order. Whilst he is showing this to the audience the* COMIC *enters.*]

COMIC: Hello, what's that you've got, a giant bingo card?

FEED 1: This is a new game I've invented. It's called, 'The guess the right number and win some money at the same time game'.

COMIC: That's what I like, a nice snappy title. What the heck does that all mean?

FEED 1: It's a way for you to win some money. Would you like to have a go?

COMIC: Yes, all right, I'll have a go. What do I have to do?

FEED 1: Well, we both put down five pounds each on the floor. Then you turn your back so that you can't see me and I point to a number on this board and if you can guess which number I'm pointing at you win all the money. Now would you like a little bet?

COMIC: Yes I'll have a bet.

[*They both put their money on the floor.*]

FEED 1: Right, now turn away. What number am I pointing at? [*He is in fact not pointing at any number.*]

COMIC: Six.

FEED 1 [*now points to number five*]: Hard luck. You were one number out. Have another go.

COMIC: All right then. One more go.

[*They both put their money on the floor again and the* COMIC *turns his back on the number board.*]

FEED 1: Off we go then. Which number am I pointing at this time?

COMIC: Number three.

[FEED *now points to number two.*]

FEED 1: Oh what a shame, you were one number out again. What bad luck. [*He picks up the money.*] Have one more go.

COMIC: I can't, I've got no more money.

FEED 1: Well I have to go to the bank to put this money in. You stay here and look after my board and see if you can get any more mugs . . . er . . . players for me and I'll cut you in on the winnings.

[FEED 1 *exits. Enter* FEED 2.]

FEED 2: What are you doing with that?

COMIC: This is a new game that I've been playing with a pal of mine but I think he was on the fiddle.

FEED 2: What's supposed to happen then?

COMIC: He points to a number and I have to guess which one it is, but he's taken all my money.

FEED 2: Well, can I help you get some of it back?

COMIC: I'll tell you what we'll do. When he comes back I'll say that you want to play and then I'll watch what number he points to and tap you on the shoulder that many times. So that way you'll win every time and I can get my money back.

FEED 2: What a good idea.

COMIC: Look out, he's coming back.

[*Enter* FEED 1.]

FEED 1: Have you found anyone else to play?

COMIC: Yes, this is him. Lord Lucan.

FEED 1: Have you got any money?

FEED 2: Yes I'll bet five pounds.

COMIC: I'll bet five pounds as well.

[*They all put their money on the floor.*]

FEED 1: Right, let's go.

COMIC: Well go on then, point to a number.

FEED 1: All right. [FEED 1 *points to number three.* COMIC *taps* FEED 2's *shoulder three times.*]

FEED 2: Er . . . number three.

COMIC: Correct. [*He picks up the money.*] Come on let's have another go. We'll make it ten pounds this time.

> [*They all place the money on the floor.* FEED 1 *points to number five and the* COMIC *taps* FEED 2 *on the shoulder five times.*]

FEED 1: Which number am I pointing at?

FEED 2: Number five.

COMIC: Correct again. [*He picks up the money.*] Come on, let's have another go.

> [FEED 1 *has realized what has been happening.*]

FEED 1: No. No more. I've finished now.

COMIC: Come on. Just because we're on a winning streak. You can't stop now.

FEED 1: Oh all right then. One more go.

COMIC: Let's bet the lot this time.

> [*They all place the money on the floor.*]

FEED 1: Here we go then. [*He releases a flap on the board which falls down over the number nine. On it is written a* 0. *He points to this* 0.]

COMIC: Oh heck. Now what? [*The* COMIC *tries to tell* FEED 2 *which number it is in mime without any success.* FEED 1 *is chuckling to himself when the* COMIC *has a brainwave. He takes a pin from his lapel and jabs* FEED 2.]

FEED 2: Oh.

COMIC: Correct again. [*They pick up the money and run off laughing, chased by* FEED 1.]

In 1677, at the Theatre Royal, Drury Lane, a pantomime was produced called *Scramouch a Philosopher, Harlequin, a Schoolboy, Bravo, Merchant and Magician.* (There's a title that trips off the tongue.) It was written by Edward Ravenscroft and the opening scene in Act Three was a schoolroom scene. This is popularly believed to be the first time that such a scene was included in a pantomime. Although the gags in this original comedy schoolroom would not be very funny if performed today, the basic idea of unruly schoolchildren baiting their not-too-bright teacher remains the basis of the schoolroom we use in our pantomimes over 300 years later.

The first schoolroom scene I appeared in was at the Theatre Royal, St Helens, in a production of *Babes in the Wood,* and when we came to the first performance I was struck by the speed at which the scene was performed. The Dame as the teacher and the Comic as the naughty schoolboy were very experienced artistes and both knew that pace is very important in a comedy routine like this. I was soon taught not to labour a gag and not to put in unnecessary words, or as our Dame, Billy Wells, put it: 'Don't make a pantomime out of a one liner.' That's arguably the best advice I've ever been given in the theatre.

I have seen many versions of the schoolroom scene over the years but the one I reproduce below contains most of the usual gags.

THE SCHOOLROOM

[*When the curtain rises on the scene the chorus of schoolchildren are running wild all over the set. They are shouting and laughing and making a lot of noise. Someone is ringing the school bell, a couple are playing conkers whilst others are playing leapfrog or just chasing around. Somebody puts a firework on the teacher's chair. The* DAME *enters.*]

DAME: Stop this noise, Be quiet and sit down. I want complete silence. [*She sits down and the firework goes off with a loud bang.*] I think the elastic's just gone in my knickers. [*They all laugh.*] Now come along scollops, I'm going to call the register. When I call out your name if you are here say 'Here Miss' and if you are not here say 'Not here Miss'. John Smith.

CHILD: Here Miss.

DAME: Ben Truman.

CHILD: Here miss.

DAME: Holsten Pils.

CHILD: Here miss.

DAME: Enough of this. It sounds more like a pub than a school. [*They all laugh and start talking.*] Order, order.

FEED: I'll have a pint of bitter.

DAME: You'll get a clock round the earhole in minute if you don't behave. [*Enter* COMIC *dressed as a schoolboy.*] Who are you?

COMIC: I'm the new boy.

DAME: You look second hand to me. What is your name, young man?

COMIC: Hammond.

DAME: Hammond what?

COMIC: Hammond Eggs. [*They all laugh.*] I'm only joking miss.

DAME: I would never have realized. What is your real name?

COMIC: My real name is Wilfred Marmaduke Hubert Pimpernel.

DAME: Very well Pimples, tell me, why are you late?

COMIC: Please miss, I got run over.

DAME: You got run over. Who ran over you?

COMIC: I ran over myself miss.

DAME: Don't be barmy, how could you run over yourself?

COMIC: Well miss, I was on my way to school this morning and I wanted someone to run across the road to get me an ice-cream, and nobody would.

DAME: So what happened?

COMIC: I ran over myself.

DAME: That is not very funny Pimples. Now, yesterday was the first day of term and you weren't here. Where were you?

COMIC: I was absent miss.

DAME: I know you were absent, boy, but you weren't here either. Where were you?

COMIC: Please miss, I've brought a note from my mum about it.

DAME: Let me see. [*See takes the note and reads.*] Dear teacher. My little boy hasn't come because he hasn't been. I've given him something to make him go and when he's been he'll come. Signed my mum. That is no excuse and what is that you've got in your hand?

COMIC: It's a lollipop. Would you like a lick?

DAME: Why thank you very much. That's very kind of you. [*She takes the lollipop and starts licking it.*] It's a very nice lollipop.

COMIC: It goes all different colours.

DAME [*still licking*]: Does it really?

COMIC: It's a good one isn't it? I was lucky to get it.

DAME: Where did you get it from?

COMIC: My dog found it in the gutter.

DAME: Ugh. You dirty little boy. Go and sit down over there. [*He sits down on a trick bench. This is a bench that has been made so that it tips up when the second person sitting on it stands up, depositing the* COMIC *on the floor.*] We are going to start lessons today with Geography.

COMIC: I don't know Geography but I know his brother Joe.

DAME: Joe who?

COMIC: Joe Ography.

DAME: Don't be cheeky. I will not have cheek in my classroom.

COMIC: Where will you have it then?

DAME: Come out here. [COMIC *stands in front of class.*] Bend over. [*He does so and she whacks him with the cane. As he sits down the* FEED, *who is sitting on the bench with him, stands up causing the bench to tip up and dump the* COMIC *on the floor. Everybody laughs.*] Sit down on the bench, not the floor. Now, what do you know about Damascus?

FEED: It kills all household germs.

DAME: Who said that?

ALL: Pimples.

COMIC: It wasn't me miss. Honest.

DAME: Don't argue. Come out here. [*He walks out and she whacks him again.*] Now go and sit down. [*The bench tips as before.*] Right. Who can tell me, what is the shape of the world?

ALL: Please teacher we don't know.

DAME: Well what is the shape of my hat?

ALL: Square teacher.

DAME: That's the shape of the hat that I wear on weekdays. What is the shape of the hat I wear on Sundays?

ALL: Please teacher, we don't know.

DAME: I've never met such a dozy lot of dimwits. It's round. Now. What is the shape of the world?

ALL [*chanting*]: Square on weekdays, round on Sundays. Square on weekdays, round on Sundays. Square on weekdays, round on Sundays.

DAME: Stooooooooop. I've never heard such a disgustipating lot of noise in my life. Who started it?

ALL: Pimples.

DAME: You are nothing but a hooligan. I should report you to the R.S.P.C.A.

COMIC: What does that stand for?

DAME: It's the Royal Society For People That Can't Act. Now come out here. [*She whacks him again and as he sits the bench tips again. As he picks himself up off the floor the* FEED *pinches his hat and throws it around the class.*] Hold it, hold it. Pimples, get your hat back and hang it up. [*He gets his hat back and draws a hook on the blackboard and hangs it on it. There is, of course, a nail in the black board where he draws the hook. After doing this he sits down with a smug look on his face.*] We will now carry on the lesson with alphabetology. What is the first letter of the alphabet?

ALL: Please teacher we don't know.

DAME: Well what do horses eat?

FEED: Straw.

DAME: Who said that?

ALL: Pimples.

COMIC: I didn't. I never said a word.

DAME: Come out here. [*Cane and bench biz as before.*] Horses eat hay. Now what is the first letter of the alphabet?

ALL: Please teacher, hay.

DAME: No. You dumb dingbats. It's hay without the aitch. Now for the last time, what is the first letter of the alphabet?

ALL [*They all chant*]: Hay without the aitch. Hay without the aitch. Hay without the aitch. Hay without the aitch.

DAME: Shuuuuut uuuuuuuuuup. This is worse than Grange Hill. What is the second letter of the alphabet?

ALL: Please teacher, we don't know.

DAME: What a well educated lot of yobs you are. I'll help you. What is that little insect that flies around my garden in the summer time flitting from flower to flower.

FEED: Hippopotamuses.

DAME: Who said that?

ALL: Pimples.

DAME: I'm fed up with you interrupting with your mouth. Come out here.

COMIC: It wasn't me. I was having a kip.

DAME: That only means you are interrupting in your sleep. Now, bend over. [*Cane and bench biz.*] We now come to the third letter of the alphabet. Which Brain of Britain can tell me what it is?

ALL: Please teacher, we don't know.

DAME: Well what do I do with my eyes?

FEED: Squint.

[*The* TEACHER *glares at the* COMIC. *He gets up without saying a word, walks over to her and bends down. Cane and bench biz.*]

COMIC: Please miss, can I go to the loo?

DAME: No you can't. You can stay behind after class and fill the inkwells.

COMIC: If I can't go to the loo can I recite a poem what I writ.

DAME: What you writ. Where's your grammar?

COMIC: She's at home with my grandpa.

DAME: She writes. He writes. We write. They write.

COMIC: All right, everybody writes. But I writ this poem.

DAME: For goodness sake come out here and tell us it.

COMIC: I've got a little bunny,
          His nose is rather runny,
          But please don't think it's funny.

FEED: 'Cos it's snot.

[*This time the* DAME *sees the* FEED.]

DAME: I saw you then. It's been you all the time. You're the one that's been causing all the trouble. Come out here at once. [FEED *comes to front of class.*] Now bend over.

FEED: Please teacher I don't know how to bend over.

DAME: You don't know how to bend over. You should have a degree in it. Pimples, come out here and show him how to bend over.

COMIC: Yes miss. I know how to do it.

[*The* COMIC *goes to the front of the class and bends over. The* FEED *bends over behind him with his hands on the* COMIC's *back. The* DAME *waves her cane.*]

DAME: This will hurt you far more than it doesn't hurt me. One, two, three.

[*On the count of three the* FEED *leapfrogs over the* COMIC *and the cane comes down on the* COMIC's *behind once again. The whole class erupts into chaos with lots of noise and music as the* DAME *chases them all off. As she ends up exhausted, lying over the desk, there is a fade to blackout.*]

There are lots of different gags that can easily be slotted into a schoolroom scene if needed. The next four are particularly well suited but they will stand on their own as well and could be used anywhere in the show.

This first one is very quick and silly but never fails to get a laugh. I don't think it's got a title so I'll call it . . .

THE CHOCOLATE GAG

[*The* TEACHER *and* COMIC *are on stage together. The* TEACHER *has two bars of chocolate in her hand.*]

DAME: I want to see what your adding and subtraction are like. What do you think of adding and subtraction?

COMIC: Well I can take it or leave it.

DAME: I mean are you any good at it? I'd better test you.

COMIC: Oh very well then. Take it away.

DAME: If you've got two bars of chocolate, one in this pocket. [*She puts bar in his jacket pocket.*] And one in this pocket. [*She puts second bar in his other pocket.*] And then I take one away. [*She takes bar out of one pocket.*] How many bars of chocolate have you got?

COMIC: Two.

DAME: No. No. No. You're not listening. I'll say it again. Give me the chocolate back.

COMIC: I knew there'd be a catch. [*He gives her the chocolate.*]

DAME: If you've got two bars of chocolate, one in this pocket [*puts it in*] and one in this pocket. [*Puts it in.*] Then I take one away. [*Takes one bar out of pocket.*] How many bars of chocolate will you have?

COMIC: Two.

DAME: How can you have two?

COMIC: I've got another bar in this pocket.

[*Pulls a bar of chocolate out of his trouser pocket.*]

This next little gag uses a blackboard, so naturally fits very well into the schoolroom scene, but I have worked it on a frontcloth and in other scenes without the Dame as teacher but if you do this, one or two lines would need altering.

THE BLACKBOARD GAG

DAME [*to* COMIC]: Why haven't you done your homework?

COMIC: Because I've had too much work to do.

DAME: What work? You don't work.

COMIC: Oh yes I do. I work very hard.

DAME: I bet I can prove that you don't work at all.

COMIC: I bet you can't.

DAME: Come here to the blackboard and I'll prove it to you. [COMIC *and* DAME *move to the blackboard*.] Now then, tell me, how many days are there in a year?

COMIC: Three hundred and sixty-five.

DAME: Correct. [*She writes it on the board*.] Now how many hours a day do you work?

COMIC: I work eight hours a day.

DAME: Eight hours a day. That's a third of a day.

COMIC: Yes that's right.

DAME: Well, three hundred and sixty-five divided by three is . . . [*Works it out on board*] . . . is one hundred and twenty-one point six. We'll knock off the point six for time spent in the toilet during working hours, so that makes it one hundred and twenty-one.

COMIC: There you are, I work one hundred and twenty-one days a year.

DAME: Oh no you don't. You don't work Saturdays and Sundays do you?

COMIC: No, of course not.

DAME: And how many Saturdays and Sundays are there in a year?

COMIC: There's fifty-two Saturdays and fifty-two Sundays.

DAME: That's one hundred and four days. Take that from one hundred and twenty-one. [*Works it out on the board*.] That leaves seventeen days.

COMIC: Well at least that's seventeen days a year that I work.

DAME: I don't think it is. Tell me do you have a holiday.

COMIC: Yes I go to sunny Margate every year.

DAME: And how long do you go there for?

COMIC: I always go for two weeks.

DAME: Two weeks' holiday, that's fourteen days. Fourteen from seventeen leaves three. [*She writes this on the board.*]

COMIC: Well all right then, I do three days' work a year.

DAME: Do you work Christmas Day?

COMIC: Of course not.

DAME: Do you work Boxing Day?

COMIC: Well no.

DAME: And do you work Easter Monday?

COMIC: No I don't.

DAME: There you are then, three from three equals nothing. As I said you don't do any work at all.

[*Black-out.*]

Another quickie that utilizes a blackboard is this next one, which is called 'Seven Thirteens'. In this gag the Comic proves to the Teacher that seven times thirteen equals twenty-eight. It seems impossible doesn't it, but this is how he does it.

SEVEN THIRTEENS

DAME: Who can tell me, what is seven multiplied by thirteen?

COMIC: I can teacher. Seven times thirteen is twenty-eight.

DAME: Seven times thirteen is twenty-eight, how do you get that answer?

COMIC: I'll show you. [*He comes out to the blackboard and writes:*]

$$13$$
$$\times$$
$$7$$

[*He then works out the sum explaining it as he does it.*] Seven times three is . . .

AUDIENCE: Twenty-one.

COMIC: Seven times one is . . .

AUDIENCE: Seven.

COMIC: Twenty-one plus seven is twenty-eight.

DAME: That's not how you do it, you turnip.

COMIC: OK. I'll do it a different way.

[*He writes seven thirteens on the blackboard thus:*]

$$13$$
$$13$$
$$13$$
$$13$$
$$13$$
$$13$$
$$13$$

[*Then he adds them up getting the audience to call out the answers with him.*] Three plus three is . . .

AUDIENCE: Six.

COMIC: Plus three is . . .

AUDIENCE: Nine.

COMIC: Plus three is . . .

AUDIENCE: Twelve.

COMIC: Plus three is . . .
AUDIENCE: Fifteen.
COMIC: Plus three is . . .
AUDIENCE: Eighteen.
COMIC: Plus three is . . .
AUDIENCE: Twenty-one.
COMIC [*Pointing to each one in turn.*]: Twenty-two, twenty-three, twenty-four, twenty-five, twenty-six, twenty-seven, twenty-eight. There you are. That proves that seven times thirteen is twenty-eight.

This following routine has been modernized somewhat by presenting it as a version of the television quiz show *Mastermind*, but all the gags remain good old pantomime gags just the same. I have worked this routine several times and can vouch for its success. This is one of the routines that I shall be using in my pantomime this coming Christmas.

MASTERMIND BRAIN OF BRITAIN

DAME: [*to* COMIC]: You really are a complete dimwit aren't you?

COMIC: I'm not a dimwit, I'm very brainy.

DAME: You, brainy? If brains were gunpowder you wouldn't have enough to blow your nose.

COMIC: I could have been on *Mastermind*.

DAME: Well why weren't you?

COMIC: I spelt the address wrong on the envelope.

DAME: I'll find out if you were good enough for *Mastermind*. Sit here. [*He sits in a chair. The lights dim except for a spotlight on his face. Music plays.*] Name?

COMIC: Dover.

DAME: First name?

COMIC: Ben.

DAME: Occupation?

COMIC: Department of Social Security . . . customer.

DAME: Chosen subject?

COMIC: How to get money without working.

DAME: You have two minutes to answer questions on how to get money without working, starting now. What do you call a narrow pathway between two mountains?

COMIC: Errrrr. Pass.

DAME: Correct. When driving along the road what should you do if the car in front of you stops?

COMIC: Errrrr. Pass.

DAME: Correct. When one footballer kicks the ball to another member of his own team, what is that manoeuvre called?

COMIC: Ummmm I don't . . . errrr. Pass.

DAME: Correct. In an exam if you score more than the minimum number of points required, what do you do?

COMIC: Errrr. Pass.

DAME: And now general knowledge. Where are the Andes?

COMIC: On the end of your wristies.

DAME: What do you know about Damascus?

COMIC: It kills ninety-nine per cent of all known germs.

DAME: Who was born in a stable and had millions of followers?

COMIC: Red Rum.

DAME: If it takes a man and a half, a year and a half, to build a wall and a half, with a brick and a half, how long would it take a Chinese accountant with a wooden leg and ginger hair to walk from Birmingham to Plymouth with a jar of marmalade on his head?

COMIC: Errrr. Four pounds twenty-seven.

DAME: Correct. If someone is described as being a sandwich short of a picnic, they are as daft as what?

COMIC: They are as daft as you are.

DAME: I'll teach you to call me daft.
    [*She starts hitting him.*]

COMIC: Oh stop. Stop. [*The bleeper goes.*]

DAME: I've started so I'll finish. [*Music Plays. Fade to black-out.*]

Here's a silly little piece of business that is usually put just before a bedroom scene. I suppose the most famous bedroom scene in pantomime is the 'Babes' Nursery' in *Babes in the Wood* where the Dame, as the Babes' Nurse, puts them to bed and the robbers break in to try to kidnap them. I have played the Nurse in this subject only twice but both times I did these gags with the babes and they seemed to work very well.

BEDTIME

[*Enter the* DAME *and the two* BABES.]

DAME: Come along you two, it's time we were all in bed.

BOY BABE: Why do we have to go to bed so early?

DAME: Well I need my beauty sleep.

GIRL BABE: Does sleep make you beautiful?

DAME: Of course it does.

BOY BABE: You must have been laying awake a lot.

DAME: Don't be cheeky. Men say I've got everything they want.

BOY BABE: You have. Muscles, hairy chest, moustache.

DAME: I've got an hour-glass figure.

GIRL BABE: Yes, but all the sand has gone to the bottom.

DAME: Never mind all this, it's time to go to dreamland.

BOY BABE: I had a dream last night. I dreamt I was eating a giant marshmallow and when I woke up half the pillow was gone.

GIRL BABE: Well I dreamt I was eating Shredded Wheat and when I woke up half the mattress was gone.

DAME: That's nothing. I dreamt I was in bed with a horse and when I woke up I was.

BOY BABE: Really?

DAME: Yes, it was a night mare.

GIRL BABE: If I go to bed early I always wake up with a pain.

DAME: Where is this pain?

GIRL BABE: Six inches above my head.

DAME: Well I'll give you a pill that will cure that.

GIRL BABE: When should I take it?

DAME: Half an hour before you wake up. Now come along, we've got to clean our teeth. I'll get the stuff. [*She exits.*]

BOY BABE: She's got teeth like stars.

GIRL BABE: Has she?

BOY BABE: Yes they come out at night.

[DAME *enters. She is holding a large toothbrush and a glass of water. She also has her mouth full of water. The three of them stand in a line. She gives the toothbrush to the* GIRL *and the glass of water to the* BOY. *The girl brushes her teeth, the* BOY *takes a mouthful of water and gargles and the* DAME *spits out the water she has in her mouth. The three of them then march off in a line.*]

Slapstick scenes have always been very popular in pantomimes and are loved by both children and adults. They are also fun for the actors to perform but generally stage managers hate them. They don't like the fact that the 'splosh' gets on the scenery, and props and furniture have to be cleaned off at each performance. If you don't keep an eye on it you'll quite often find that the amount of 'splosh' gets less every performance so that there is less mess to clean up. This can only spoil the scene and if you are going to include a slapstick scene then do it properly with as much 'splosh' as you can get. Most 'splosh' is made from shaving soap with a little glycerin added and then whisked until good and thick. Once, however, I appeared in a show where the director insisted that the custard pies were made from flour, water and size and I had to take about a dozen of them at each performance. There is never enough time to clean it all off properly and this stuff used to set hard during the rest of the show and you'd spend hours picking it out of your ears and eyebrows and so on. This next gag though, is a fairly easy one to do, for although it involves breaking eggs they don't mess up the scenery, just the Comic's hairstyle.

THE EGG GAG

[DAME, COMIC *and* FEED *enter.*]

COMIC: I have just written a beautiful piece of poetry.

DAME: You write poetry?

COMIC: Yes I'm very good at it.

FEED: Let's hear it then.

DAME: Is it clean?

COMIC: Of course it's clean.

DAME: Well come on then, we'd better hear it.

COMIC: OK. This is it:

> Dear little birdie in the tree.
> Dear little birdie flying free.
> Dear little birdie I love thee.
> Won't you send some love to me.

[*An egg falls down and smashes on his head.*] Ow. That was awful! Look at all this mess.

DAME: That was the birdie sending you some love.

COMIC: Well it should have sent hard-boiled love.

FEED: I know some poetry.

COMIC: Oh good. [*To audience*:] Let him get some love.

FEED: Do you want to hear it?

COMIC: Yes, go on then.

FEED: There was a handsome sailor . . .

COMIC: Hold on. Hold on. Can't you do one about a bird?

FEED: I don't know one about a bird.

COMIC: Well do the one I've just done.

FEED: I can't remember it. How did it go?

COMIC: Dear little birdie in the tree.
　　　Dear little birdie flying free.
　　　Dear little birdie I love thee.
　　　Won't you send some love to me.
　　　[*Another egg falls on his head.*] Oh heck, what a mess.
　　　[*The* FEED *exits laughing.*]

COMIC [*to* DAME]: Don't you know any poetry?

DAME: Yes, I do. Would you like me to recite it?

COMIC: Is it about a bird?

DAME: Yes it is.

COMIC: Oh good. Go on then, tell us it.

DAME: Dear little birdie . . .

COMIC [*to audience*]: It's the same one.

DAME: 　I'll start again.
　　　Dear little birdie in the tree.
　　　Dear little birdie flying free.
　　　Dear little birdie I love thee.

COMIC: Yes. Yes. [*Getting all excited*].

DAME: Send some love to him from me.

　　　[*Another egg falls on the* COMIC's *head. He chases her off.*]

A lot of slapstick scenes, but by no means all of them, take place in the kitchen. Kitchens are excellent places for comedy as they open up all sorts of chances to juggle plates, throw food around and generally make a mess of everything. Over the years I have seen many different kitchen scenes and there are probably enough variations on the theme to fill a book but I have decided to include just three of them as they encompass every kind of comedy – verbal, visual, slapstick and knockabout. All three are different, fast and funny, but above all traditional. This first scene starts off as a gentle cookery lesson and quickly degenerates into pure mayhem.

THE KITCHEN SCENES

[*This scene involves just two people, usually the* COMIC *and the* DAME. *On stage, set centre, is a large table. On it is a mixing bowl in which is a prepared lump of dough; behind the bowl is a long sausage of dough about three feet long with a tennis-ball-sized piece next to it. To the side of the kitchen table is another small table on which is set a goldfish bowl and water and a sliver of raw carrot representing a goldfish. The other props needed in this scene will become obvious as we go along. Always make sure that the dough you are using is freshly made as stale dough not only looks bad but won't work as well either.*]

[*Enter* DAME *and* COMIC.]

DAME: Come along, I want you to help me with some cooking.

DAME: I love cooking. What are we going to make?

DAME: Let's bake a cake.

COMIC: Right. What shall I do?

DAME: You go and get the ingredients.

[*The* COMIC *exits and returns with a little open box about the size of a shoe box.*]

COMIC: Here they are. Look at them all, eating away like there's no tomorrow. Are these greedy enough for you?

DAME: What are you talking about? What are they?

COMIC: Well you asked for greedy ants.

DAME: I said ingredients, not greedy ants. Go and get me a little flour.

COMIC: Right. A little flower. [*He exits and comes back with a rose.*]

DAME: What's that?

COMIC: You said get a little flower. So I got one.

DAME: Not that kind of flower. What sort is it anyway?

COMIC: It's a chrysanthemum.

DAME: No it's not, it's a rose.

COMIC: It's a chrysanthemum.

DAME: It's a rose.

COMIC: It's a chrysanthemum.

DAME: All right. Spell chrysanthemum.

COMIC: Errrrrr. It's a rose.

DAME: Stop messing about. Now, I need some currants. Oh dear I forgot to buy some. I'm sure I haven't got any.

COMIC: Yes you have.

DAME: I thought I was out of them.

COMIC: No I know where there's some currants. I'll get them for you. [*He exits and returns with some currants in his hand.*] Here they are, lovely currants. [*He tips them into the mixing bowl.*]

DAME: Well that's good, I didn't think I had any. [*She puts some of them in her mouth.*] I love currants, where did you find them?

COMIC: I found a secret store of them, hidden in the back of the rabbit hutch.

DAME [*spitting out currants*]: You horrible little horror. [*She takes the dough out of the bowl and slams it down on the table.*]

COMIC [*pointing at dough*]: I say, do you knead the dough?

DAME: Of course I need the dough, do you think I'm doing all this for nothing? I'm skint.

COMIC: I don't mean need the dough. I mean knead the dough. [*He sticks his finger in the dough.*]

DAME: Don't put your dirty fingers all over the dough. I don't want germs on my food. Look at it, it's all grubby now. [*She spits on it and rubs it on her pinny.*] This table is none too clean either. [*She wipes the table with the dough then dusts the table legs with it and ends up wiping the floor with it.*] That's better, I can't stand a dirty kitchen. [*She puts the dough back in the mixing bowl.*] I need some more flour now. [*She pours more flour in the bowl.*] Get me some water will you?

> [COMIC *puts his hand into the goldfish bowl and pulls out the carrot. He looks at it and says:*]

COMIC: Excuse me. [*He then pours some of the water from the goldfish bowl into the mixing bowl. Then he says to the fish*]: Thank you very much. [*Puts it back in bowl.*]

DAME: That'll do. That'll do. Let's put this in the oven. [*She puts dollop of dough in the oven.*] Now, I think we'll make a sausage pie. Where's my sausages? [*She grabs her string of sausages off the table and walks away with them. The* COMIC *is leaning on the other end of the sausages and they stretch as they are made from rubber.*] Hey, get off my sausages will you? [*He lets go of the sausages and they hit the* DAME *in the rear.*] Do stop mucking about.

COMIC: Come on then. Put the sausages in the baking tin. [*She puts the sausages in the tin and one of them stands upright. As she pushes it down another sausage on the other side of the tin rises up. The* COMIC *pushes this one down and the first one comes up again. They carry on with this business for a little while until the* DAME *eventually picks up a gun and shoots the sausage, which falls down.*]

[*N.B. To prepare the sausage tin take a large baking tin and fix a wooden sausage inside it at each end. A wire handle is attached to each sausage and goes through to the outside of the tin enabling the* DAME *and* COMIC *to raise the sausages on cue.*]

DAME: Quickly, I'll put these in the oven before they escape. [*She does so.*] Now what else would you like me to make you?

COMIC: What I'd really really like is roly-poly pudding. It's my favourite.

DAME: It's funny you should say that. Here's one I prepared earlier. [*She picks up the long sausage-shaped piece of dough and hands it to the* COMIC.]

COMIC: Well isn't this lovely? It reminds me of my old school scarf. [*He puts the dough around his neck and throws the end round as you would a scarf. This end hits the* DAME *in the mouth. She has secretly picked up the tennis-ball-sized piece of dough and as she puts her hands up to her mouth she puts the dough in it. The impression given is that the* COMIC *swings the dough round his neck, hits the* DAME *in the mouth and a piece breaks off and sticks in her mouth. She makes noises and gesticulates to the* COMIC. *He pulls the piece of dough from her mouth and she mimes that her false teeth are embedded in it. She mimes pulling them out of the dough and putting them back in.*]

DAME: Will you stop messing about?

COMIC: I'm sorry, I'm sorry. I've gone off roly-poly pudding anyway. Especially since half of it got stuck in your gob. I'll tell you what, let's have dumplings.

DAME: Dumplings it shall be. Watch this. [*She lays the roly-poly pudding out on the table and picks up an axe.*] Roly-poly pudding. [*She chops the pudding into about ten pieces very quickly.*] Dumplings.

COMIC: Cor . . . they're good aren't they? Hey I've just had an idea. Let me show you how good I am at cricket.

DAME: What do you mean? What are you doing with my dumplings? [*The* COMIC *picks up a bucket which is behind the table and scoops all the dumplings into it. Already hidden in the bucket are a dozen or so 'dumplings' made of cotton wool.*]

COMIC: Come on. I'll bat, you bowl. [*He gives the* DAME *the bucket of dumplings and picks up a frying pan to use as a bat.*]

DAME: OK. If you insist, but I'm not world class.

COMIC: You're not even third class. Just chuck the dumplings. [*She bowls the cotton-wool dumplings at him and he hits them into the audience. They get the audience to throw them back to them and the* DAME *then picks up another pan to help the* COMIC *hit them back. When they have played this for a while the* DAME *notices smoke coming from the oven.*]

DAME: Quick, look, my cake is burning. Help me save it. [*They rush up to the oven and as they get to it the oven explodes and takes off like a rocket. They both watch it fly out.*]

[*Black-out.*]

The second kitchen scene is almost certainly the youngest of the three, although some of the gags included are bound to be very old. The main prop, which the whole scene hinges on, is a radio, which probably means that the main part of the routine dates from the 1930s, so at over sixty years old this is the baby of the three.

KITCHEN SCENE NUMBER 2

[*The radio is placed prominently on a table at the back of the set with the usual kitchen table a few feet in front of it. On the kitchen table is a mixing bowl containing a large piece of dough, two eggs, one of which is blown, a milk bottle painted white, a rolling pin, an old fashioned egg-whisk and a pistol. Under the table is an axe and set off stage is a rabbit on a long piece of fishing line. One more important prop is a speaking tube fixed somewhere on the set. As in the previous kitchen scene this one involves just the* COMIC *and the* DAME.]

DAME: Right, it's time I started cooking dinner and you can help me.

COMIC: All right I'll help. What shall I do first?

DAME: You can help me to make a pie.

COMIC: Lovely. What sort of pie? I know, how about a kate and sidney pie.

DAME: No I don't think so. Hey what about a nice rabbit pie?

COMIC: Yes, let's. I like rabbit pie. It's just like *Watership Down*, you've read the book, you've seen the film, now eat the pie.

DAME: Go and get me a rabbit then. Oh and make it a nice humpty back one.

COMIC: Why do you want a humpty back rabbit?

DAME: It helps hold the pastry up in the middle.

> [*The* COMIC *exits and re-enters with a rabbit which has a fishing line attached that goes to offstage. While he has been doing this the* DAME *has picked up an axe from under the table.*]

COMIC: Here it is. One funny bunny. [*He places it on the table.*]

DAME: I shall prepare the rabbit. [*She raises the axe as if to chop its head off and counts.*] One, two ... [*The rabbit is pulled on the line and moves about a foot along the table. They watch this move then the* COMIC, *without saying a word, puts the rabbit back in position.*

DAME *raises the axe and counts as before.*] One, two . . . [*The rabbit moves again.*]

COMIC: I think it's got the jitters.

DAME: Well so would you have. I'll have one more go. I'll catch it on the hop. [*She raises the axe again and counts.*] One, two, three. [*On three she brings down the axe and the rabbit shoots off stage.*]

COMIC: It's done a bunk. We'll have to think of something else for dinner. What can we have now?

DAME: I know. We'll make an omelette. Get me an egg.

[*The* COMIC *picks up an egg and places it in front of her.*]

COMIC: There you are, one egg.

DAME: Now beat it.

COMIC: If that's what you want.

[*He starts to exit.*]

DAME: Where are you going?

COMIC: You told me to beat it.

DAME: I didn't mean beat it, you dozy dinner helper, I meant beat the egg. You beat it with an egg-whisk. [*She hands him the whisk.*]

COMIC: Well why didn't you say. [*He hits the egg with the whisk and smashes it all over the table, making a lot of mess.*]

DAME: Hey, hey, hey, what do you think you're doing, you messy little monkey. You've ruined my kitchen. Look at it, it looks like a bomb's hit it.

COMIC: I'm sorry, I got carried away.

DAME: You'll be carried away unconscious if you don't watch it.

COMIC: I'm very, very, very, very sorry. I'll clear it up immediately if not sooner. [*He wipes the egg off the table with one hand and puts all the mess into his other hand.*] You're angry with me aren't you?

DAME: Well what do you expect? You've made a mess all over my M.F.I. kitchen.

COMIC: Don't be angry with me. I've cleared it all up and I've said I'm sorry.

DAME: I don't know about that.

COMIC: Please.

DAME: Well . . . I don't know.

COMIC: Friends again?

DAME: All right, friends again.

COMIC: Shake on it. [*He offers her his hand, which is full of the eggy mess and they shake.*]

DAME: You horrible little yob. Look what you've done to me. Wait till I get my hands on you. You'll pay for this. [*She chases him around the stage.*]

COMIC: Keep away from me. Don't you touch me. [*As he runs round the table he picks up the blown egg which he threatens her with.*] Be careful, I've got another egg here.

DAME: Don't you throw that at me.

COMIC: They call these chucky eggs.

DAME: Why do they call them chucky eggs?

COMIC: Because you can chuck them. [*The* DAME *is downstage at this point with the* COMIC *upstage. He throws the blown egg at her, she ducks, and the egg goes into the audience. The* COMIC *speaks to the audience member who got hit by the egg.*] I'm so sorry missis, you should have kept your mouth shut.

DAME: Stop messing about. That's an egg we've lost now. [*To audience member.*] You couldn't cough it up could you?

COMIC: Well what do we do now?

DAME: Go and get me some flour.

COMIC: Where do I get the flour from?

DAME: There is a speaking tube over there which connects you to Sainsbury's. You pick it up and say into it, 'Can you send up some flour?' and you'll get it.

COMIC: I just say, 'will you send up some flour,' and I'll get it, will I?

DAME: Oh yes, you'll get it all right.

[*The* COMIC *walks over to the speaking tube, which consists of a piece of plastic tubing with a funnel fixed to the end of it. The funnel is hooked onto the set with the tube going off stage. The funnel has talcum powder in it. He speaks into the funnel.*]

COMIC: I say, you down there. Can you send up some flour? [*Someone off stage blows through the tube and the talcum powder goes all over the* COMIC's *face.*] Very funny, I don't think.

DAME [*Laughing*]: You know why that happened, don't you? You didn't say please. Try it again.

COMIC: I'll have another go. [*He speaks into the tube.*] Can you send up some flour please? [*He gets it in the face again.*]

DAME: You're still doing it wrong. Say, can you send up some flour please, and get your head out of the way.

COMIC: OK. I'll try that. [*He speaks into the tube again.*] Can you send up some flour please and get your head out of the way. [*Once again he gets the talcum powder in the face.*] It's not fair.

DAME: No, no, no, you don't say get your head out of the way, you get it out of the way.

COMIC: Well, why didn't you say? [*He speaks into the funnel again.*] Can you send up some flour please? [*He gets his head out of the way and the talc blows into the air. He speaks into the funnel again.*] Ya, you missed me. [*The talc then blows into his face again.*] I'm fed up with this.

DAME: Never mind the flour. Pass me that milk.

    [*He picks up the milk bottle and up-ends it. Of course nothing comes out as it's painted white.*]

COMIC: Hey look, it's frozen.

DAME: Well of course it is. It comes from a Frisian cow. Now stop this mucking about and knead this dough. [*She gets the lump of dough from the mixing bowl and puts it on the table.*]

COMIC: Do what?

DAME: I said knead the dough.

COMIC: If you say so. [*He climbs onto the table and kneels up and down in the dough.*]

DAME: What do you think you're doing?

COMIC: I'm kneading the dough.

DAME: Not like that. Really, you'll drive me out of my mind.

COMIC: Well, you won't have far to go will you?

DAME: I know what we'll do. We'll turn on the radio to see if the daily recipe is on yet.

    [*She turns on the radio.*]

RADIO: Good morning housewives.

COMIC: I'm not a housewife.

RADIO: I wasn't talking to you.

COMIC: So sorry, I'm sure.

RADIO: Today I'm going to tell you how to make a steak pudding.

DAME: Steak what?

RADIO: You heard. Now first of all you take a large basin, large basin, large basin . . .

DAME: It's stuck in the groove.

COMIC: I'll fix it. [*He hits the radio with the rolling pin.*]

RADIO: Thank you.

COMIC: It's a pleasure.

RADIO: Now go and get a pound of steak.

DAME: It's in the other room, I'll go and get it. [*She exits.*]

COMIC: I'll play a trick on her. I'll change the radio station. [*He does so.*]

RADIO: Hello. This is Radio Four with a talk on football.

[*Enter* DAME *with a large piece of steak.*]

DAME: I've got the steak, what do I do now?

RADIO: The first thing we must do is to warm up. If we don't warm up properly we could break a leg or something.

DAME: How can you break a leg making a steak pudding?

COMIC: Just do as the radio says. They know what they're talking about.

RADIO: Let's run around and throw it to one another.

COMIC: Come along. Do as the radio says.

[*They run around the stage throwing the steak from one to another.*]

DAME: This is barmy.

RADIO: Now let's kick it to one another.

DAME: If that's what the man says. [*They kick the steak to one another.*] What now?

RADIO: Now I want you to throw it in the air and head it.

DAME: Am I hearing that right?

COMIC: Of course you are. Now, I'll throw it and you head it.

[*He takes the steak and throws it to the* DAME *who heads it. They do this two or three times.*]

RADIO: Have you done that?

DAME: You can see we have.

RADIO: No I can't, I'm a radio, you twerp.

DAME: I'll throttle that radio in a minute.

COMIC: Don't get excited. It'll be a lovely pudding when it's finished. What shall we do now?

RADIO: I want you to put it on the floor and dribble.

DAME: Put it on the floor and whattle?

RADIO: Not whattle, dribble.

DAME: If that's what you want . . . [*She puts it on the floor and starts to dribble over it.*]

COMIC: He doesn't mean that kind of dribble. He means this kind. [*He starts to dribble the steak around the stage. As he does so the radio speaks.*]

RADIO: That's right. That's right. Now shoot.

DAME: Do what?

RADIO: Shoot. Shoot. [DAME *picks up the pistol from the table and shoots the steak three times.*]

DAME: That's the daftest way I've ever heard of making a steak pudding.

RADIO: Steak pudding? I'm teaching you how to play football.

DAME [*to* COMIC]: That was you changed that radio station. Wait till

I get my hands on you. [*She picks up the rolling pin and the chase music starts as she chases him around the stage.*] Come here you little horror. I'm going to give you what for.

COMIC: I'm not staying here so that you can knock me into the hereafter.

DAME [*still chasing him*]: What does that mean?

COMIC: Well, if you're here after what I'm here after, you'll be here after I'm gone. [*He runs off stage and the* DAME *runs up to the radio.*]

DAME: This is all your fault. Take that. [*She hits the radio with the rolling pin.*] And that. [*She hits it again.*] And that. [*As she hits it the third time the radio explodes.*]

[*Black-out.*]

This last kitchen scene in our trio of culinary delights is more messy than the other two with nearly everyone, including the audience, getting cakes thrown at them. It involves one more person along with the Dame and the Comic and therefore gives a little more scope for slapstick effects. One very important point to remember when delivering a custard pie into someone's face is to use a cupped hand to hold the pie. A flat hand under a thin cardboard plate smashing into your nose is not the best way to improve your looks.

KITCHEN SCENE NUMBER 3

[*The scene is set with a large kitchen table and two chairs, one of which is behind the table and the other to one side of it. On the table is a large piece of dough, a dustpan and brush, a solid egg made of stone, some real eggs and a few unglazed plates. Set under the table are two large custard pies, a rolling pin, a mallet and a saw.*]

[DAME *and* COMIC *enter together.*]

DAME: Come along. It's time to cook something for dinner.

COMIC: Do you want me to help then?

DAME: That's very kind of you. Would you roll out the pastry while I go and get my apron on. You'll find the rolling pin under the table. [*She exits.*]

COMIC: Right. Where's the rolling pin. I'll soon get this sorted out. [*Music starts. He gets the rolling pin from under the table and starts rolling out the dough at a great speed. After a while he starts hitting the dough with the rolling pin in an attempt to flatten it. He then pulls out a large mallet from under the table and hits the dough with it. After this he gets a wood saw from under the table and saws the edges of the dough off. When the dough is all nice and flat the* DAME *enters.*]

DAME: What a lovely job you've made of it. I couldn't have done better myself. [*She gets behind the table.*] Mind you this table looks none too clean does it? I can't stand a dirty kitchen. [*She wipes the table using the dough as a duster and picks up things from the table and dusts them.*] When you are working in a kitchen you must make sure your utensils are clean.

COMIC: That's exactly what I say. I must say though, that pastry's a bit grubby isn't it?

DAME: Do you think so? [*She holds it up.*] I'll soon clean up. [*She puts it on the table, spits on it and brushes it off with the dustpan and brush.*] There that's better. Now you season it.

COMIC: Do what?

DAME: Season it.

COMIC: If you insist. [*He sneezes on the dough.*]

DAME: What do you think you're doing?

COMIC: You said sneeze in it.

DAME: Not sneeze in it, you great dollop, I said season it.

COMIC: Oh, I'm so sorry.

DAME: Get me an egg.

COMIC: Hey, shall I show you a new trick? It's how to catch an egg on a plate.

DAME: Oh yes. Come on, show me how to do it.

COMIC: You do it like this.

[*He throws the egg in the air and catches it on the plate. This is done by bringing the plate up to meet the egg as it comes down, thereby lessening the impact as the egg hits the plate.*]

DAME: That's really clever. Can I have a go?

[*She throws the egg high in the air then turns round to pick up a plate from the table. The egg, of course, smashes on the floor.*]

COMIC: You don't do it like that. You must get them both in your hands at the same time.

DAME: Well why didn't you say? [*She picks up an egg and a plate.*] You mean like this?

COMIC: That's right. Now throw it up in the air. [*She throws both the egg and the plate in the air together. They both smash on the floor.*] Not both of them together, you only throw one.

DAME: I'm sorry. I've got it now. [*She picks up an egg and a plate, throws the plate in the air and tries to catch it on the egg. Once again the plate smashes on the floor.*]

COMIC: You're not safe to be let out. Listen to me. You take the egg in one hand, the plate in the other and you throw the egg in the air. Do you get it?

DAME: Got it.

COMIC: Good. Then do it.

DAME: I'll do it. [*She picks up an egg but this time it's the solid egg. She then picks up the plate, throws the solid egg in the air and*] *catches it on the plate but, of course, being solid, it still smashes the plate.*]

COMIC: You're a disaster. I'm going to get rid of the rest of these plates so you can't smash them. [*He picks up a pile of cardboard plates which were hidden under the real ones.*]

DAME: Where are you going to put them?

COMIC: Out here. [*He throws the plates, one by one, into the audience.*]
[*Enter* FEED *with a large gooey cake in each hand.*]

DAME: What's that?

FEED: I've brought you a present, a couple of cakes.

DAME: How very, very, kind of you. Put them down here. [*He puts them both on the table.*]

FEED: [*to* COMIC]: I've made one for you as well.

COMIC: How very, very, philanthropic of you.

DAME: I think he's swallowed a dictionary.

FEED: I'll go and get it. [*He exits and returns with a very large gooey cake.*]

DAME: Isn't this lovely? It's looking like the Women's Institute bring-and-buy.

COMIC [*taking cake from the* FEED]: It's smashing. I'll put it here. [*He puts the cake on the chair which is set to the side of the table.*]

DAME: That's really kind of you. I won't eat them now, I'll keep them in lieu.

COMIC: That's a funny place to keep a cake. If someone pulls the chain they'll go clean round the bend.

FEED: I'm so tired after all that cooking. I must sit down. [*He is standing in front of the chair that has got the cake on it. As he absent-mindedly goes to sit down the* DAME *speaks to him, stopping him from sitting in the cake.*]

DAME: I say.

FEED [*getting up*]: Yes?

DAME: Did you bake all these cakes?

FEED: Yes I did. [*He goes to sit again.*]

DAME: How long did it take you?

FEED [*getting up again*]: About three hours.

[*He goes to sit again but the* COMIC *has been watching the action and just as the* FEED *is about to sit on the cake the* COMIC *pulls the chair to the side so that he will sit on the floor. But the chair is now behind the* COMIC *and as the* FEED *falls he puts his arms* out which has the effect of pushing the COMIC *down onto the chair and into the cake.*]

COMIC: Oh what a mess. [*He shows his cake-covered rear to the audience.*]

DAME [*laughing*]: I think you've got a little behind in your work.

COMIC: I'll teach you to laugh at me.

[*He picks up one of the cakes on the table and advances towards the* DAME *who backs away. The* FEED *is now standing behind the* DAME *laughing at the situation. The* COMIC *goes to throw the cake at the* DAME; *the* DAME *ducks and the cake hits the* FEED *in the face. At this the* COMIC *laughs and sits on the chair at the back of the table. He now has the last cake right in front of him on the table.*] I love to see somebody get it right in the face.

DAME/FEED: Do you really? [*They are standing either side of him. They reach down under the table and both bring out a cake. They both raise them as if to throw.*]

DAME: I say.

COMIC [*nervously, still seated.*] What do you want?

DAME: Have this one on me. [*They both go to throw the cakes but the* COMIC *ducks, pushing his own face into the cake on the table. As he ducks he throws up his arm pushing the* FEED'S *cake into the* FEED'S *face. This leaves the* DAME *holding the last cake.*] Now, what shall I do with this one?

[*She walks towards the audience looking for a victim. At last she spots someone and throws the cake into the audience. It is only then that we realize that her cake is made from a lightweight solid foam and drops into the stalls. Or it could be on elastic so that she can get it back. As the cake goes into the audience there is a black-out.*]

Aladdin is probably the second most popular pantomime subject after *Cinderella*, although *Snow White* seems to be creeping up in the popularity stakes over the past few years. The story of Aladdin comes originally from the *Arabian Nights* stories and was first performed as a pantomime in 1788 at the Theatre Royal in Covent Garden. The dame, Aladdin's mother, is called Widow Twankey but this wasn't always the case. She started off being called the widow Ching Mustapha, then went through three or four variations of this before arriving in the 1860s at Twankay, which was the name of a type of tea. Over the years Twankay has evolved into Twankey, the name now used in every production.

In every modern production of *Aladdin* Widow Twankey runs a Chinese laundry and this scene is usually the main comedy scene in the show. As with most of the gags and sketches there are several versions of the laundry and most Dames add their own favourite bits of business, but I've chosen to reproduce this version as it contains most of the usual 'washing' gags and lots of visual ones as well. The scene involves Widow Twankey, her son Wishee Washee and the two Chinese policemen.

WIDOW TWANKEY'S LAUNDRY

[*Set on stage in this scene are a washing machine or old-fashioned copper, a trick mangle with rollers that lift up, allowing someone to pass right through it, and a washing tub on a stand or table.* WISHEE *enters with a big pile of washing in his arms which wobbles about dangerously. He runs downstage to the audience and the pile of washing falls over towards them. It is in fact all tied together with a wire right through the middle of it so that he keeps hold of the pile.*]

WISHEE: Mum. Mum, where are you?

    [*Enter* TWANKEY.]

TWANKEY: Here I am, Wishee. I've been hanging the washing on the line.

WISHEE: But mum, we haven't got a washing line.

TWANKEY: We have now, look. [*She has a washing line with washing hanging on it wrapped around her body. She twirls across the stage unwinding the washing as she goes. (Someone offstage is holding*

*the end of the line.) She twirls right across the stage and off the
other side. The line is then held, out of sight, on both sides of the
stage.* TWANKEY *runs around the back of the set and twirls back on
to the stage with a second line of washing wrapped around her.
This comes to an end when she reaches the centre of the stage.*]

WISHEE: Oh mum, what a way to dry the washing.

TWANKEY: Well, I've got such a lot of work to do. I've got a little
behind.

WISHEE [*looking behind her*]: Oh no you haven't.

TWANKEY: Cheeky thing.

WISHEE: I've finished all my work now, mum. Can I have some money
to go to the pictures?

TWANKEY: Money to go to the pictures. My mother never gave me
money to go to the pictures.

WISHEE: Well you must have had a rotten old mother.

TWANKEY: How dare you. I had a better mother than you've got.
[*She realizes what she has said.*] Oh, silly me.

WISHEE: Oh come on mum, give me some money.

TWANKEY: Serpently not.

WISHEE: Very well then, that's it. From now on you and I are total
strangers. You go my way and I'll go yours. [*He pulls a face at
her.*]

TWANKEY: Did you pull a face at me?

WISHEE: No I didn't. [*To audience.*] Did I, boys and girls?

TWANKEY: Oh yes he did. [*Audience shout back.*] Let me tell you
something my boy. When it comes to pulling faces I can pull a
worse face than you.

WISHEE: Yes, but look at the start you've got.

TWANKEY: Don't you be cheeky to me or I'll stop your pocket money.

WISHEE: You don't give me any pocket money.

TWANKEY: Well I'll start and then stop. Now come here and help
me with this washing. [*They pull the tub forward and both stand
behind it as* TWANKEY *starts to rub the clothes.*] I nearly won the
pools last week you know.

WISHEE: Did you really mum?

TWANKEY: Yes I did. My homes were all right, my aways were all
right but my draws let me down. [*She pulls a pair of tatty old knickers
from the tub.*]

WISHEE: I see you are doing washing for the best people in town,
mum.

TWANKEY: The best people in town?

WISHEE: Yes. [*He pulls out a local football team's shirt with holes in it, and names them.*]

TWANKEY: It's got holes in it.

WISHEE: I know, they're the holes in their defence.

TWANKEY [*pulls out large pair of bloomers and sings to the tune of 'wouldn't it be loverly' from* My Fair Lady]: All I want is some knickers like these, to keep me warm from my neck to my knees . . .

WISHEE: Hey look mum. [*Pulls out very large pair of Y-fronts.*] Bernard Manning's. [*Or names any other very large man in the news.*]

TWANKEY: Look at these. [*Pulls out tiny pair of men's pants.*] Ronnie Corbett's. [*Or any other small man.*]

WISHEE [*Pulls out corset*]: What are these mum?

TWANKEY: Give them here. [*She plays the corset as if playing an accordion and sings to the tune of 'This is my lovely day'.*] These are my lovely stays. These are the stays I will be wearing the day I'm dying.

[*There is a loud knocking at the door.*]

WISHEE: Someone's ringing the bell.

[*Enter the two* POLICEMEN.]

POLICEMAN 1: We have come to arrest Aladdin.

[WISHEE *runs and hides behind* TWANKEY.]

TWANKEY: Aladdin's not here.

POLICEMAN 2: Then we will arrest him for G.B.H.

[*Pointing at* WISHEE.]

WISHEE: G.B.H. You mean grievous bodily harm?

POLICEMAN 1: No. Getting behind her.

POLICEMAN 2: We have been informed that your copper is bunged up.

TWANKEY: I know two other coppers that should be bunged up.

POLICEMAN 1: If you've got an unbunger we will help you to unbung it.

WISHEE: I'll get the unbunger mum. [*He gets a sweep's brush or similar on a very long bendy handle which he waves about over the heads of the audience.*]

POLICEMAN 1: Come along then, we'll help you to put it in the copper. [*They get the long brush and feed it in to the copper.* TWANKEY *is bending down by the window watching this. The brush goes into the copper and a second one comes in through the window and hits* TWANKEY *in the rear. She screams and picks up a bowl of soap suds.*]

TWANKEY: How dare you interfere with my person? [*She puts the bowl of soap over the* FIRST POLICEMAN'S *head.*]

POLICEMAN 1: Look what you've done to me. You've ruined my uniform.

WISHEE: Quick mum, put him in the copper. That'll clean him up.
[TWANKEY *and* WISHEE *bundle the* POLICEMAN *into the copper. The* SECOND POLICEMAN *is jumping up and down during all this, getting more and more angry.*]

POLICEMAN 2: What have you done to my mate? I'm going to arrest the pair of you. [*He chases them round the stage.* TWANKEY *and* WISHEE *get one either side of the mangle.* TWANKEY *turns the handle and the* POLICEMAN *dives right through the mangle.*]

WISHEE: Oh heck mum. Look what we've done. Turn the handle the other way, let's get him back.

TWANKEY: Good idea Wishee. [*She turns the handle the other way and a flat cut-out policeman comes back.*] Oh look Wishee, he's been on a diet.

WISHEE: Oh mum, we've forgotten the copper in the copper.

TWANKEY: You're right. Let's get him out quick.
[*They run to the copper and open the door. A little child dressed in a copy of the policeman's uniform runs out.*]

BOTH: Blimey, he's shrunk. [*The* LITTLE POLICEMAN, *waving his truncheon, chases them around the stage, through the audience to off.*]
[*Black-out.*]

The Drill Routine, which comes next, is a classic. It is usually in *Dick Whittington* or *Robinson Crusoe* but I have also seen it used in *Snow White*, *Mother Goose* and other, not so popular subjects, like *Sinbad the Sailor*.

As I've stated elsewhere in this book, the first pantomime I appeared in was *Sinbad the Sailor* and I well remember being banished to the theatre bar with the other comics in the show, to rehearse the Drill Routine. As so often happens there was nothing of this in the script save for the short note 'Drill Routine as set' which meant absolutely nothing to me at the time. In the bar we talked through the routine several times for an hour or so and as we walked back to the dressing rooms I remarked to one of the other comics that I would be more sure of the routine next time we came to rehearse it. 'Next time?' he said. 'You'll be lucky. The next time we do this will be on the opening night.' And it was! Talk about baptism of fire. I have never forgotten that opening night at the Palace Theatre, Plymouth. I stood in the wings, terrified that I wouldn't remember my words. The overture finished, the curtain rose to reveal the stalls and royal circle packed with children and their parents and as was customary in those days in Plymouth, the gallery packed with sailors and their girlfriends. The fairy entered and uttered her first line: 'I am the sailors' fairy friend.' The whole gallery erupted into laughter, whistles and catcallls for what seemed like hours before we could carry on. However, carry on we did and eventually got to the Drill Routine that follows. It's a very flexible routine and can involve three, four or five people. The version I relate here is set on the ship with the captain taking the drill.

THE DRILL

[*Enter* CAPTAIN, COMIC, DAME, MATE, FEED.]

CAPTAIN: Now then you lot. I think we ought to have some drill. We'll use mops instead of guns until you know what you're doing. Mr Mate, give out the mops. [MATE *gives everybody except* CAPTAIN *a mop.*] Right, you lot, fall in. [*They all rush to the side of the ship as if to jump overboard.*] What do you think you're doing?

FEED: You said fall in.

CAPTAIN: I didn't mean fall in like that. I meant fall in over here, blockheads.

ALL: Fall in here. Fall in there. I wish he'd make up his mind. [*They all mutter.*]

CAPTAIN: Shut up. Now then, attenshun, at ease, shun ease, shun ease, shun ease.

DAME [*throwing down her mop*]: I wish you'd make up your mind.

CAPTAIN [*indicating her mop*]: Pick that up.

DAME: No.

CAPTAIN: Pick it up.

DAME: No.

CAPTAIN: I said pick it up.

DAME: I said no.

CAPTAIN: Will you pick that up?

DAME: No I will not.

CAPTAIN: Please pick it up.

DAME: Errr. No, I don't want to.

CAPTAIN: Just for me.

DAME: Errrrrrrrrr no.

CAPTAIN: Oh very well then, don't. [*He walks away, then suddenly turns and shouts.*] Pick it up. [*The* MATE *jumps into the* DAME'S *arms.* FEED *picks up the mop and hands it to* DAME.] Stand at ease. Stand easy. [COMIC *leans on his mop with his legs apart. The* DAME *kicks the mop through his legs causing him to fall over.*] What are you doing down there?

COMIC: Getting up.

CAPTAIN: Get up and get in line. Now, from the right, number! [*They all start dancing.*] What do you think you're doing? I said number.

COMIC: Oh. We thought you said rumba.

CAPTAIN: Pay attention. From the right, number!

FEED: One.

DAME: Two.

COMIC: Two.

CAPTAIN: Again.

FEED: One.

DAME: Two.

COMIC: Two.

CAPTAIN [*to* COMIC.] Aren't you one?

COMIC: No, but I'm a bit worried about him.

[*Pointing to* FEED.]

CAPTAIN [*Pointing to* FEED.] Who are you?

FEED [S*cottish accent*]: I'm very well thanks and who are you?

CAPTAIN: Bah. Come along now. Squad. Close up. [*The* DAME *lifts up the front of her skirt.*] Not that way.

DAME: Oh, you mean this way. [*She turns round and lifts the back of her skirt to reveal an 'L' plate sewn on the back of her knickers.*]

CAPTAIN: Stand up woman. What do you think you are doing.

DAME: I was only doing what you said.

CAPTAIN [*shouting*]: Shut up.

DAME: There's no need to shout at me. I'm doing my best. [*She dissolves into tears.*] It's not fair. I am trying. You shouldn't be nasty to me.

CAPTAIN: I will carry on. Who knows anything about navigation?

MATE: I do. My father was a navvy.

CAPTAIN [*to* COMIC]: What's your name?

COMIC: Nosbert Buttock.

CAPTAIN: Well Mr Buttock, I'm going to make a sea-dog out of you. What do you say to that?

COMIC: Woof. Woof.

CAPTAIN [*short and sharp*]: Squad.

ALL: [*short and sharp*]: Yes.

CAPTAIN: Squaaaaaaaaaaaaaaad!

ALL: Yeeeeeeeeeeeeeeeees!

CAPTAIN: Present arms! [*They run over to him and offer him the mops.*] That's not how you present arms. I'll show you. [*He takes a mop from the* COMIC.] It's like this. [*He presents arms properly.*] One and two and three and four. [*He throws the mop on the floor.*] That's the way to do it. Now. Squad. Present arms!

ALL: One and two and three and four. [*They all throw their mops on the floor.*] That's the way to do it.

CAPTAIN: If you lot don't behave I'll hang you from the top of that mast there. [*Indicating right.*]

COMIC [*Indicating left*]: I prefer that one over there.

CAPTAIN: Shut up. Now then, squad, shoulder arms. [*They shoulder arms but* DAME *puts her mop on the wrong shoulder.*] No not on that shoulder, put it on this one. [*Patting his own left shoulder.* DAME *puts her mop on the* CAPTAIN'*s shoulder.*] Not there. Put it where he's got his. [*He points to the* COMIC'*s shoulder. The* DAME *now puts her mop on the* COMIC'*s shoulder. The* CAPTAIN *grabs her mop from the* COMIC'*s shoulder and puts it in position on her left*

• 116 •

shoulder. He is by now beside himself with rage and shouts at her.]
Put it there. Put it there.

DAME: Well why didn't you say?

CAPTAIN [*to* COMIC]: If we were attacked at sea, what steps would
you take?

COMIC: Bloomin' great big ones.

CAPTAIN: None of you look as if you are fit enough to defend anyone.
We'll do some exercises. Follow me. [*He runs on the spot.*] One
two, one two, as if you were riding a bicycle. One two, one two, as
if you were riding a bicycle.

ALL [*joining in running on the spot*]: One two, one two, as if you were
riding a bicycle. One two, one two, as if you were riding a bicycle.
[*The* DAME *stops and leans on her mop. The others carry on.*]

CAPTAIN: What do you think you're doing? [*The others stop.*]

DAME: I'm free-wheeling. [*They all laugh.*]

CAPTAIN: Bah and bah again. Squad attention. [*They all stand to
attention.*] Left turn. [*They all turn left except for the* COMIC *who
turns right and faces the* DAME. *She grabs her chance and gives
him a quick kiss.*]

COMIC [*turning the right way*]: Yuk and double yuk.

CAPTAIN: Quiiiiiiiiiiiick . . . [*They anticipate his command and lift their
legs ready to march.*] Wait for it. Wait for it. March. [*Music plays.
They march around the stage and salute the audience as they exit.*]

One of the most famous slapstick scenes in pantomime is the one where the comics try to decorate the parlour. Paste, paint and paper get everywhere but where they're supposed to be and everyone gets in a glorious mess. There are records of this routine going back over two hundred years and it's still to be found in dozens of productions every year. It is important that you make sure you have plenty of time to get cleaned up after this scene. I've seen people in slapstick scenes who are obviously trying to avoid getting too messy and it doesn't work as well. Remember: the more mess the bigger the laughs. A word of warning, though: make sure the mess doesn't get out of control. There's nothing worse than suddenly seeing a great dollop of coloured paste heading out into the audience and landing on somebody's best clothes. One version of this scene that I took part in ended with one half of a very well-known double act filling a bowler hat with the paste and forcing it on his partner's head, causing all the paste to squirt out of a hole in the top of the hat; a very funny tag, except for one night when they got the hat at the wrong angle and all the paste shot into the orchestra pit and covered a lady trombone player. She complained long and loud so at the next performance the said double act purposely aimed the hat at her and squirted. Unfortunately their aim wasn't good and a man in the front row got covered in pink paste.

DECORATING THE PARLOUR

[*For this routine the props needed are as follows: a large paste table and a pair of steps are set upstage. On the table is a large paste brush and underneath it are a bucket of paste and two rolled pieces of wallpaper, each about two metres in length. The rest of the props can be placed anywhere convenient. After a couple of rehearsals you will know the best place to set the props to suit your action. Apart from the bucket of paste set under the table you will need three more buckets full of paste and three buckets of paint, one bucket without a bottom and a bucket with a hole in the side small enough to block with your finger. Use the usual splosh made of shaving soap for the paste and a thinner version coloured with food colouring for the paint.*]

[*Enter* DAME *and* COMIC.]

DAME: It's about time we decorated this room, it hasn't been done for years.

COMIC: Don't worry about it, I'll help you, we'll have it done in a tick.

DAME: Well OK then, but we mustn't make a mess or there'll be trouble.

COMIC: Stop worrying, there won't be any mess. Where shall we start?

DAME: Just hold this bucket and I'll pour the paint in.

[*She gives him a bucket to hold which has no bottom in it. When she pours the paint in it goes all over his shoes.*]

COMIC: What do you think you're doing?

DAME: Oh I'm so sorry. I've splashed your shoes. I'd better use this other bucket.

[*She fills a second bucket with paint. This one has a small hole in the side near the bottom over which she puts her finger to stop the paint dribbling out. She climbs a step ladder. The* COMIC, *who is wearing a bowler hat, stands at the foot of the steps. He takes his hat off and holds it out while he ad libs chat about the job. The* DAME *takes her finger off the hole and the paint pours into the* COMIC's *hat. He puts his hat on and gets a soaking.*]

COMIC: What are you playing at? I'm getting covered in muck here.

DAME: Never mind, the colour suits you.

COMIC: I don't care about the colour, I care about getting covered. [*He shakes the paint off.*]

DAME: Be careful. We mustn't make a mess. [*She comes down the steps.*] Pass me that bucket of paint there. [*He hands her a bucket of paint which she cradles in her arms.*] Now, get that paste ready and hold on to these steps.

[*The* COMIC *places a bucket of paste at the bottom of the steps. He holds on to the steps and as the* DAME *climbs them the paint splashes out of her bucket all over the* COMIC *at the bottom of the steps.*]

DAME: You're getting in a heck of a mess down there. Can't you be a bit more careful? [*She climbs down the steps and puts her foot in the bucket of paste. The bucket gets stuck on her foot.*] Don't just stand there looking with your eyes, help me get this off. [*He pulls the bucket off her foot and they both fall over.*]

COMIC: I think we should do the papering first. It's not so messy is it?

DAME: That's the best idea you've had today. You can paste the paper.
[*He puts the paper on the table and goes to paste it but every time he stops to get paste on the brush the paper rolls up. After a few attempts at this he lifts his leg on to the table and holds the paper down with his foot while he pastes it.*]

DAME: What do you think you're playing at?

COMIC: What do you mean?

DAME: You're pasting the wrong side of the paper. You should paste the underside.
[*The* COMIC *immediately starts to paste the underside of the table.*]

COMIC: Is that right?

DAME: No it isn't. Now take this paper and stick it on the wall.
[*He climbs the steps with the roll of paper unrolled in front of him so that as he climbs the steps he treads on the paper which tears off. By the time he gets to the top of the steps he is left with a tiny piece of paper which he dabs on the wall.*]

COMIC: How's that?

DAME: At this rate it should only take us three years to do this room. Come here, I'll show you how to do it. [*She gets a fresh roll of paper and unrolls it on to the table.*] Now, hold on to the end of that paper and don't you dare let go of it. I don't want it rolling all over the place.
[*He holds the end of it by kneeling at the end of the table and holding the paper down with his fingers. His face is almost level with the paper. She pastes the paper without looking at what she is doing and consequently pastes his face as well. As she holds the paper up as if to put it on the wall he lifts her skirt, revealing her knickers, and wipes his face on it.*]

COMIC: I've got paste in my eyes now.

DAME: Well don't wipe it all over my skirt. I've got another three payments on this.

COMIC: Never mind your rotten skirt, I've got blooming paste everywhere and it's all your fault.

DAME: My fault is it? Well, if you've got paste everywhere then a little more won't hurt you, will it?
[*She goes to the paste bucket and gets her hands full of paste. She walks towards him with her hands out as if to slap them in the* COMIC'*s face but he claps her hands together causing the paste to go all over her. She goes back to the bucket and gets another handful of paste and rubs it in his face. He then gets a*

handful of paste and rubs it in her face. She picks up a bucket of paste and pours it into his trousers. He gets a bucket of paste and pours it into the neck of her jersey. As she looks down he slaps the front of her jersey and all the paste goes in her face. She takes his bowler hat and fills it with paste. There is a small hole in the top of the hat so as she forces the hat down on to his head the paste squirts out of the top.]
[Black-out.]

I should think that anyone who has ever been in a pantomime has taken part in a ghost gag. It must be the oldest gag on record. We know that even the ancient Greeks had ghosts in their plays and you can't get much older than that. The reaction it gets from the children in the audience is tremendous. The ghost only has to appear to start the children shouting and screaming 'It's behind you' and the noise doesn't cease until the gag is over and the ghost has disappeared for the last time. I once saw a ghost accidentally fall into the orchestra pit as he tried to exit and half the audience started to climb into the pit to get to him. I dread to think what would have happened if the orchestra hadn't fought off the children and they had got hold of the poor ghost.

Although this is a very simple, straightforward gag, there are several versions of it, so I have written the usual routine first and then added three alternative versions.

THE GHOST GAG

[*At the start of the gag there are four people on stage, the* DAME, *the* COMIC *and two others.*]

COMIC: I don't like the look of this place.

FEED 1: Nor do I.

FEED 2: It feels creepy.

DAME: I bet it's haunted.

COMIC: I want to go.

DAME: You should have gone before you came out.

COMIC: I mean I want to go home.

DAME: Well you can't, so there.

FEED 1: I hope we don't see a ghost.

COMIC: Well if a ghost does appear perhaps the boys and girls will shout out and warn us.

DAME: Will you do that boys and girls? If you see the slightest sign of a ghost shout out loud so we'll know.

FEED 2: What are they going to shout?

COMIC: They can shout zim.

DAME: Why do they want to shout zim?

COMIC: Because then we'll know it's 'im.

FEED 2: I've heard that if we sing that'll keep the ghost away.

DAME: Your singing would keep anything away.

FEED 1: What shall we sing?

COMIC: I know, let's sing Ten Green Bottles.

[*They all start to sing. The* GHOST *enters and walks straight across the stage behind the actors and off the other side. The audience shout.*]

COMIC [*to audience*]: Did you say something?

ALL: What?

A ghost.

Where?

Over there. [*Pointing.*]

We'll go and have a look then.

[*They walk round to look for the* GHOST *who has, by now, gone.*]

DAME: There's nothing there.

COMIC: We'll sing again.

[*They start to sing again an the* GHOST *walks across the stage and off the other side again.*]

COMIC [*to audience*]: Did you say something?

ALL: What?

A ghost.

Where?

Over there. [*Pointing.*]

We'll go and have a look then.

[*They walk around again but still don't see the* GHOST.]

DAME: There's nothing there.

COMIC: We'll sing again then.

[*They start to sing and this time the* GHOST *enters and stands behind* FEED 2. *He taps him on the shoulder.* FEED 2 *turns and sees the* GHOST *and is chased off by it. The rest carry on singing all through this, ignoring the shouts of the audience.*]

COMIC [*to audience*]: Did you say something?

DAME: Where's Feed 2?

ALL: What?

A ghost.

Where?

Over there. [*Pointing.*]

We'll go and have a look then.

[*They all walk round together and find nothing.*]

DAME: There's nothing here.

COMIC: We'll sing again.

[*They sing.* GHOST *enters and frightens off* FEED 1.]

COMIC: Did you say something?

DAME: Where's Feed 1?

ALL: What?

    A ghost.

    Where?

    Over there. [*Pointing.*]

    We'll go and have a look then.

    [*As usual they walk round and find nothing.*]

DAME: There's still nothing there.

COMIC: We'll keep on singing.

    [*They sing. The* GHOST *enters, taps the* DAME *on the shoulder and exits.*]

DAME [*to* COMIC]: Stop tapping me while I'm trying to sing.

COMIC: I didn't tap you.

DAME: Well who did?

ALL: What?

    A ghost.

    Where?

    Over there. [*Pointing.*]

    We'll go and have a look then.

    [*This time they walk round in opposite directions.*]

DAME: I can't see anything.

COMIC: I think they're messing us about. We'll keep on singing.

    [*They sing again. The* GHOST *enters and this time frightens off the* DAME.]

COMIC: Did you say something?

 [*He looks around.*]

Where's the Dame gone?

What?

A ghost.

Where?

Over there. [*Pointing.*]

I'll go and have a look then.

    [*He walks around and finds nothing.*]

    I'd better sing it again, all on my own.

    [*He sings. The* GHOST *enters and stands next to him. The audience shout and the* COMIC *stops singing. He is by now very frightened.*]

D-d-d-d-did you s-s-s-say something?

What?

A ghost.

Where?

Over there. [*Pointing.*]

I'd better have a look then.

    [*He very slowly turns until he sees the* GHOST. *He screams and is chased round the stage and off by the* GHOST.]

    [*Black-out.*]

Here are three other versions of the ghost gag which I think are all as good as the original. They are very useful if you should be appearing at the same venue every season but want to include a ghost gag in every pantomime.

VARIATIONS ON THE GHOST THEME

1. In this adaptation the gag runs through as in the main version except that the Comic is frightened off by the Ghost before the Dame goes, leaving her on stage alone. She sings and the Ghost enters and stands next to her. The Ghost strokes her leg and she assumes it's the Comic and tells him to stop messing about. This happens two or three times and when she eventually turns to face him the Ghost sees her, screams and runs off.

2. In this version the running order of the gag is exactly the same as in the main layout except that every time the Ghost enters he gets taller. To start off use a child in the ghost costume, then a small adult for the second entrance, a large adult follows for the third entrance, after which a false head and shoulders attached to a very long costume is used. The head and shoulders are fixed to a pole and the actor inside the costume can make the Ghost taller every time he enters by simply raising the pole.

3. This final version runs through as usual until the Comic and Dame are the only people left on stage. The Ghost enters and stands in between them. When they say 'We'll go and have a look then' they both turn in and see the Ghost, who runs away. They chase him around the stage, into the auditorium, across the front of the stage and back onto it. The ghost runs off stage and the Dame and Comic follow. When they are out of sight of the audience they grab a dummy ghost which is dressed the same as the real one. The dummy is fixed to a line which is secured from above the stage. They carry the dummy on, as if they've just caught the real Ghost, count to three and throw him into the audience. A black-out comes before the dummy starts to swing back on to the stage. In the black-out they grab the dummy and carry it off.

Still on the subject of 'Ghosties and ghoulies and things that go bump in the night'. This next sketch can really bring the house down. Many years ago when variety acts would tour their own scenery with them, a certain well known double act built their act around this next sketch and earned a good living from it for many years. It does though rely on having a good set built as most of the laughs come from visual 'prop' gags and from the set itself, but it is well worth the expense as it can be fitted into any pantomime subject and is guaranteed to be the funniest scene in the show.

I first performed this sketch in a pantomime in Belfast with the great comedian Frank Carson and we often got told off by the stage manager for causing the show to overrun. It wasn't that we put extra business into the sketch but at some performances the laughs were so long and loud that the running time extended by up to five minutes or more.

THE HAUNTED BEDROOM

[*The haunted bedroom set is really two bedrooms. A central half wall splits the stage in half. In this wall is a trick door which is both a normal and a revolving door. The door and frame will revolve if the door is pushed but if the handle is turned the door will open in the usual way. In one room is a bed which is on castors and can be pulled backwards through a hole in the rear wall of the set. Above this bed is a moose head or similar with an open mouth and to the side of this room is a chest of drawers, which must be side on to the audience. The second room has a grandfather clock and a bed that tips up into the wall. Various other props are used but they will become obvious as the sketch unfolds. The scene involves the* COMIC, *the* DAME, *a* GHOST *and a* GORILLA.]

[*Enter* DAME.]

DAME: What a creepy old bedroom. It looks like an M.F.I. reject. I don't fancy sleeping in here. Just look at it.

[*Enter* COMIC *in nightshirt.*]

COMIC: It's a bit spooky isn't it? It's enough to make your nightshirt curl.

DAME: Well we've got no choice, we've got to sleep here, so we'll have to put up with it. What time is it?

COMIC: There's a clock here, let's see.

[*They both look at the grandfather clock. The hands go whizzing round accompanied by loud whizzing and clanging noises. Their heads go round with the hands as they try to tell the time.*]

COMIC: It's ninety-two minutes past fifteen.

[*The clock stops at three o'clock and strikes three times.*]

DAME: No it's not. It's one o'clock three times. We'd better get ready for bed.

COMIC: I wonder what's through here.

[*He opens the door and they both walk through to the other room.*]

DAME: That's good, it's another bedroom. You can have this one and I'll have the other.

[*She goes back into her bedroom.*]

COMIC: OK, you can have the Slumberland, I'll have this. [*He bangs the bed and it is solid.*] Oh heck, bed and board.

DAME: Don't forget to clean your teeth.

COMIC: Good job you reminded me.

[*He cleans his teeth with a giant toothbrush and takes a mouthful of water from a glass which is set on the chest of drawers. He looks around for somewhere to spit the water but can find nowhere. He pulls out the top drawer of the chest, which is about six feet in length and spits into it before closing it again.*]

DAME: Are you in bed yet?

COMIC: No, I've got to look for something first. [*He feels about under the bed.*] I know it's here somewhere. They always keep them here. Ah here it is. [*He pulls out a nightcap which he puts on then gets into bed.*] I'm in bed now, are you?

DAME: I'm just going to get undressed. [*She undresses, taking off several petticoats and many pairs of knickers. Then she puts on her nightgown, which was lying on the bed, and gets into the bed.*]

COMIC: Are you in bed now?

DAME: Yes I am. Are you all right?

COMIC: Yes, I'm in bed and everything's all right. [*He is sitting up in the bed with the moose head right above him. The moose's tongue comes out and pulls off his nightcap which it then throws on the floor.*]

Help. Help. Help. [*He jumps out of the bed. The DAME jumps out of bed and runs through the door, opening it properly.*]

DAME: What's the matter?

COMIC: Something threw my cap on the floor.

DAME: Don't be silly, there's nothing here. Now get back into bed.
[*She walks back through the door and climbs into her bed. The* COMIC *puts his hat on and gets into his bed.*]

COMIC: I'm all right now. Nighty Nighty.

DAME: Pyjama, Pyjama.
[*The moose's tongue again pulls off his nightcap but this time it holds on to it. The* COMIC *jumps out of bed again.*]

COMIC: Help, help, help.
[*The* DAME *jumps out of bed and rushes through the door to him.*]

DAME: What on earth's the matter?

COMIC: Something's pulled my cap off again.

DAME: Well where is it?
[*They look around his bed for his cap but cannot find it.*]

COMIC: Where's my cap gone? [*To audience.*]

DAME: Look, it's in the Moose's mouth.

COMIC: He must have been trying to eat it.

DAME: Don't be silly, it just got hooked up. I'll get it out.
[*She takes his cap from the moose's mouth.*] Thank you Mr Moose.

MOOSE: That's quite all right.

DAME: Don't mention it. Now get back into bed and go to sleep.
[*The* COMIC *is standing there shaking.*]

COMIC: Th . . . Th . . . Th . . . That Mmmmmmmmmmmoose spoke to you.

DAME: Don't be daft, of course he didn't. Now get into bed.
[*She goes through the door and into her bed. As the* COMIC *lies down his bed slides through the wall and back out again.*]

COMIC: Help, help, help. [*He jumps out of bed and runs to the door. He pushes the door and runs round and round with it before ending up in the* DAME'*s room.*]

DAME: What's wrong with you now?

COMIC: When I said goodnight to you my bed slid into the wall and when I tried to come through the door it went round and round.

DAME: Don't be ridiculous. [*She gets out of bed and walks through the door. He follows her.*] There's nothing wrong with this door, it works all right and your bed is still there.

COMIC: Well it wasn't a minute ago.

DAME: Oh go to bed and go to sleep. [*She goes to her bed and the* COMIC *climbs into his.*] Nighty, nighty.

COMIC: Pyjama, pyjama. [*As he lies down again the bed slides into the wall and out again.*] Help, help, help. [*He jumps out of the bed, runs to the door which again goes round and round with him before depositing him in the* DAME's *room.*]

DAME: Oh not again. What's up now?

COMIC: It's happened again. The bed went into the wall and the door went round and round.

DAME: I think you're dreaming all this. [*She checks the door and bed again.*] There's nothing wrong with them. Now go to bed.

[*He gets into his bed and the* DAME *gets into hers. As he is sitting in bed a giant spider comes down in front of his face then flies out again.*]

COMIC: What was that? [*Audience shout: 'A spider.'*] Oh no it wasn't. [*Audience shout: 'Oh yes it was,' etc.*] Well I'm taking no notice. I'm going back to sleep. [*The spider comes down again.*] Help, help, there's a spider in my room.

DAME [*Walking into his room*]: You're not scared of a little spider are you? [*She sees the spider hanging there, screams and runs. The door goes round and round and she ends up in her room. She jumps into her bed.*] I don't like this at all.

[*As they both sit in their beds a* GORILLA *enters, walks across the front of both rooms and off the other side. They follow it with their eyes, then both dive under the covers. As this happens the* COMIC's *bed slides through the wall. When it comes back the* GORILLA *is in the bed with him. The* COMIC *sees the* GORILLA *and screams. The* GORILLA *jumps off the bed and runs off. The* COMIC *runs into the* DAME's *room round the front of the set.*]

COMIC: Quick, quick, quick, there's a gorilla.

DAME: You can't come through that way, you've just walked through the wall. [*They both fall about laughing, then the* COMIC *walks back the way he came and enters again through the door.*]

COMIC: There, are you happy now?

DAME: If a thing's worth doing, it's worth doing properly.

COMIC: Now I've forgotten the script.

DAME: Look. The only way we're going to get any sleep is for us to change rooms. You sleep in my room and I'll sleep in yours.

COMIC: Good idea. Nothing's happened in this room. I'll have this bed. [*He climbs into her bed whilst she walks through the door and gets into his.*] Nighty, nighty.

DAME: Pyjama, pyjama. [*As she lies down there is a ghostly laugh and her bed slides into the wall. She screams, which makes the* COMIC *sit up in bed. Then her bed slides slowly back into the room without her in it but with the* GHOST *there. It gets up and walks through the door, spinning it as it goes. It enters the* COMIC's *room and gives a blood curdling laugh. The* COMIC *dives under the covers and as he does so his bed tips up into the wall.*]

[*There is a slow fade to black-out as the* GHOST *stands and laughs over weird music, thunder and lightning.*]

No pantomime would be complete without a comedy love scene with the Dame. Traditionally the Dame is either a widow or a spinster and is always looking for a man. In some subjects she does end up with a man of her own; I've known her marry King Rat in *Dick Whittington* and the Squire in *Mother Goose*. In a production of *Dick Whittington* that I appeared in one Christmas, the Captain and Mate were, according to the script, both after marrying me. During one scene I climbed on a table to escape their advances and grabbed hold of a chandelier hanging above me, to swing across the stage. As I swung they were supposed to jump up and grab my skirts which would fall off revealing my voluminous knickers. At one performance they somehow managed to get their hands inside the waistband of not only my skirts but my tights and briefs as well and as they pulled, everything came down around my ankles and I was left hanging from the chandelier with my naked rear swinging before the audience like a carcass in a butcher's window. Needless to say I didn't marry either of them at the end of the show.

A LITTLE LOVE SCENE

[*Enter* COMIC *and* DAME.]

COMIC: Well come on then, how about a little kiss?

DAME: Men say I'm a lovely kisser.

COMIC: Where did you learn how to kiss?

DAME: I used to syphon petrol out of army lorries.

[*He puts his arm around her.*]

DAME: I like your arm, it's so big and strong.

COMIC: I know. I grew it myself.

DAME: Don't squeeze so hard.

COMIC: Why not.

DAME: You're pushing all the blood up to my head.

COMIC: You smell nice.

DAME: I should do, I've just sprinkled myself with toilet water.

COMIC: I tried that once but the seat fell on my head.

DAME: When I was younger I used to be the belle of the ball.

COMIC: What happened?

DAME: Somebody pinched my clanger.

COMIC: Have you had boyfriends before?

DAME: Oh yes. My last boyfriend was very bowlegged. In fact he was so bowlegged if I wanted to sit on his lap I had to put a plank across.

COMIC: Is he the only one?

DAME: No. I had another boyfriend, but he died through drinking milk.

COMIC: How did that happen?

DAME: The cow fell on him.

COMIC: Tell me what sort of a man are you looking for?

DAME: I want a man who'll pick me up, whirl me round and drain me dry.

COMIC: You don't need a man, you want a spin dryer.

DAME: I could have married the mayor you know. But I messed it up.

COMIC: Really?

DAME: Yes. I went to this posh party and the mayor was there in his chain of office and I had this very low-cut dress on with a rose in the cleavage. The mayor walked over to me and he said 'If I kissed your rose would you blush?'

COMIC: And what did you say?

DAME: I said 'If I pulled your chain would you flush?'

COMIC: I feel a song and dance coming on.

[*They sing a chorus of a well-known song and start to dance. After a couple of steps the* COMIC *swings his arm round and hits the* DAME *in the face.*]

COMIC: Oh dear, I'm dreadfully sorry.

DAME: You hit me right across the face.

COMIC: Do let me kiss it better.

DAME: If you insist. [*She puckers up, pushing her face out in a horrible grimace. The* COMIC *kisses her on the cheek.*] Oh thank you. [*The music starts again and they carry on dancing. The* COMIC *stands on her foot.*]

DAME: You trod on my foot.

COMIC: I'm terribly sorry. Do let me kiss it better.

DAME: Well if you insist. [*The* DAME *lifts her foot and the* COMIC *kisses it better.*] Thank you so much.

[*The music starts again and they carry on dancing. This time after a few steps they bump bottoms.*]

COMIC: Oh madam, I'm terribly sorry.

[*The* DAME *positions herself for him to kiss it better.*]

DAME: I'm waiting.

COMIC: You can kiss that better yourself.

　　[*They go into the last chorus of the song and exit at end.*]

Of all the scenes in all the pantomimes I've appeared in over the years my favourite scene from a performer's point of view has to be the shop scene from *Dick Whittington*. The main comedy part of the scene is usually between the captain, the mate and the Dame who, in this subject is Sarah, the cook. The captain and mate come into the shop where Sarah is working, to order some ship's stores and, as might be expected, between the three of them the whole thing turns into complete chaos.

Over the years, as you can imagine, there have been many gags written for this scene and there are many versions of it in evidence every Christmas but this is the one that I do whenever I am asked to appear in *Dick Whittington*. This is the best of the old gags, and one or two of my own, put together in the way I like to work them.

THE SHOP SCENE

[*This set is a typical shop scene with a large counter set upstage centre. On the counter stands a large birthday cake, made of gooey cream, the bigger the better. Next to the cake is a bolt of shot silk, a starting pistol and a french stick. Under the counter is a pair of shoes, a prop side of bacon, a large round of cheese and a sack of tea.*]

> [SARAH *the cook is dusting the shelves when we first see her, singing to herself.*]

SARAH: Oh I do like looking after the shop. For one thing it means I don't have to go far to do my shopping. Now what can I get for Alderman Fitzwarren's tea tonight? I think I'll just bang the shelf and see what falls off. [*She bangs the shelf and a tin of cat food falls off.*] Oh dear, cat food again! Still he'll never know the difference, I'll put it in a pie. I've given him cat food every day this week and he hasn't noticed. Mind you last night he nearly ricked his neck, trying to lick his back.

> [CAPTAIN *and* MATE *enter.*]

CAPTAIN: Are you in charge here?

SARAH: Of course I'm in charge. I am Alderman Fitzwarren's manager and his chef de-la-cuisine.

MATE: We don't care who your cousin is, we just want serving. [*He sticks his finger in the cake on the counter and licks it.*]

SARAH: I'll serve you one in a minute and get your finger out of that cake. It's a special order for someone's birthday. Now then Captain, what can I get you that's got twopence off?

CAPTAIN: I just want some stores.

SARAH: Wouldn't you like my special offer?

MATE: No, just some stores. [*He puts his finger in the cake again and licks it.*]

SARAH: Don't touch that cake. [*She hits him with a French stick that is on the counter.*]

CAPTAIN: We need some things for our voyage.

SARAH: What can I get you?

CAPTAIN: Do you sell floor polish?

SARAH: Yes, we do.

MATE: Do you sell paraffin?

SARAH: Yes, we do.

CAPTAIN: Do you sell soap?

SARAH: Yes, we do.

MATE: Well, wash your hands and get me a quarter of ham. [*He sticks his finger in the cake.*]

SARAH: I've told you before not to touch that. [*She hits him with the French stick.*]

CAPTAIN: I want some shot silk.

SARAH: Certainly. Here it is. [*She holds up a bale of cloth.*]

MATE: That's not shot.

SARAH [*She picks up the starting pistol and shoots it*]: It is now.

CAPTAIN: How much is it?

SARAH: Ten pence a hole. Of course that's the wholesale price.

MATE: What will you take off for cash?

SARAH: Everything except my earrings. [*The MATE sticks his finger in the cake.*] And don't touch that cake. [*She hits him with the French stick.*]

MATE: I want the cheapest pair of shoes in the shop.

SARAH: You're wearing 'em.

CAPTAIN: Sarah, you're so cheeky, have you no scruples?

SARAH: No but I could order you some. [MATE *sticks his finger in the cake and she hits him again.*] I have told you before with my mouth, don't touch that cake.

CAPTAIN: Really, I can't find words to express my disgust.

SARAH: I could sell you a dictionary.

MATE: I want a pair of shoes, size nine.

SARAH: Here, try these. [*She gets a pair of shoes from under the counter. He tries them on.*]

MATE: They're a bit too tight.

SARAH: Try it with the tongue out.

MATE [*Speaks with his tongue sticking out.*] They're still too tight. [*He sticks his finger in the cake again and she hits him again.*]

SARAH: Will you not touch that cake?

CAPTAIN: I need a side of bacon, Sarah.

SARAH: Here you are. One side of bacon. [*She hands him a side of bacon from under the counter and he starts to exit.*]

CAPTAIN: How silly of me, Sarah, it's not bacon I want, it's cheese.

SARAH: What a silly billy you are. Here's some cheese. [*She takes the bacon off him and gives him a cheese. He goes to exit.*]

CAPTAIN: Oh dear, I'm just not with it today, am I? It's not cheese I want, it's tea.

SARAH: What a soppy sailor you are. Here's some tea. [*She takes the cheese off him and gives him a sack of tea. He goes to exit.*] Just a minute, Captain, you haven't paid me for the tea.

CAPTAIN: But I gave you the cheese for the tea.

SARAH: Yes, but you didn't pay for the cheese.

CAPTAIN: Well of course not, I gave you the bacon for the cheese.

SARAH: I know, but you didn't pay for the bacon.

CAPTAIN: Well we didn't have the bacon did we?

SARAH: Oh no, of course not ... [*To audience*] I think I've been diddled here and I didn't feel a thing.

MATE: Would you like this sweet, Sarah?

SARAH: Oh, thank you very much. [*He hands her a sweet which she puts in her mouth.*]

MATE: Do you like it?

SARAH: Yes I do, I think it's very nice.

MATE: Well our dog didn't. He licked it twice and left it.

SARAH: You little horror. [*She goes to hit him round the back of the head but he ducks and puts his face into the cake. Chase music starts playing here and SARAH starts chasing the CAPTAIN and MATE around the shop.*]

SARAH: I've told you a dozen times not to touch that cake. Get out of my shop.

[*As she chases them out the CAPTAIN picks up the bacon, tea and cheese and runs off.*]

To end this compilation of all the oldest and funniest pantomime gags in captivity, I have decided to include some running gags. Now these are not gags that you tell whilst running round the stage, as some may think, although perhaps that's not a bad idea, because it is harder for an audience to hit a moving target. These are silly gags that the Comic repeats on nearly every entrance he makes, cumulating, sometimes, in a tag which he does on his last entrance. The first one is the most usual.

HI YA KIDS

On the Comic's first entrance, when he introduces himself to the audience, he tells the children that everytime he comes out he will shout, 'Hi Ya Kids', and they must shout back 'Hi Ya Jack', or whatever his name is. He rehearses it three times with them. After they shout back the first time he tells them he couldn't hear a thing; after the second time he tells them he could just hear a mumble but after the third time he can hear all of them. He then shouts out 'Hi Ya Kids' everytime he comes on to the stage and ensures a rousing reception for every entrance.

HI DE HI

This one has become very well known since it was adopted as the title for the popular television sitcom. It's exactly the same routine as the one above except that the Comic shouts out 'Hi De Hi' and the audience shout back 'Ho De Ho'.

CUDDLY TOY

This running gag costs the price of a good cuddly toy at each performance but it is well worth the investment. At his first entrance the Comic introduces the children to his cuddly rabbit, dog, or whatever and stands it in the corner of the stage where everyone can see it. He tells them that if anyone goes near it or touches it during the performance they must call him. Of course it is planned that certain characters do try to take the animal and when the children call the Comic on he chases them away. At the end of the show he gets a small child up to help him, usually with the song sheet, and he then makes them an offer. They can either have the cuddly toy or a signed photograph of himself to take away with them. Of course they want the toy but many of them don't like to say so for fear of hurting the Comic's feelings. Naturally they end up with the photograph and the toy.

THE FLOWER

In this gag the Comic enters carrying a flower in a pot. He places it in the corner of the stage and tells the audience that he keeps forgetting to water it, so everytime he comes on will they shout out 'Water the Plant'. He places a watering can next to the plant and when they shout out he waters it and to everyone's astonishment it grows and grows until by the end of the show it nearly reaches the ceiling. What in fact has happened is that when he first puts the plant in the corner he hooks a piece of fishing line on to the plant which goes right up the proscenium arch and down the inside where it is pulled up everytime the plant is watered. The plant must have a great long stem hidden in the pot. This takes a bit of arranging but is well worth the effort.

DON'T PRESS THE BUTTON

Hanging on the proscenium arch for this gag is a large bell push with a notice underneath saying 'Do not push this button'. During the Comic's first entrance he tells the audience that if they see anyone go to push the button they are to shout for him. When, throughout the show, various people go to push it and the children shout for him, he runs on and chases them off. At the end of the show he explains that he doesn't know what the button does and he is going to push it to find out. The children will shout for him not to but he pushes it regardless and runs to the other side of the stage to watch what happens. There is a whirring and buzzing sound as if a great clock is about to strike and a giant hammer, made of foam rubber, appears on the side of the stage he is standing on and hits him on the head, knocking him over.

THE HANKY GAG

The last of these running gags involves several handkerchiefs of various sizes. When the Comic first enters he tells the audience that he has a very bad habit of sniffing and he needs their assistance to help him to stop. He asks them to shout out 'Hankie' every time he sniffs, when they do this he pulls out his handkerchief and wipes his nose. Everytime he enters he sniffs and the audience shout out 'Hankie' but the handkerchief he pulls out of his pocket gets bigger every time. The last time he does this, usually in the finale, the handkerchief is as large as a big tablecloth and is guaranteed to get a big laugh.

FOR YOUR OWN GAGS

FOR YOUR OWN GAGS

FOR YOUR OWN GAGS

FOR YOUR OWN GAGS